Images and Options
in the Language Classroom

CAMBRIDGE LANGUAGE TEACHING LIBRARY
A series of authoritative books on subjects of central importance for all
language teachers.

In this series:

Teaching and Learning Languages *by Earl W. Stevick*

Communicating Naturally in a Second Language – Theory and practice in
language teaching *by Wilga M. Rivers*

Speaking in Many Tongues – Essays in foreign language teaching
by Wilga M. Rivers

Teaching the Spoken Language – An approach based on the analysis of
conversational English *by Gillian Brown and George Yule*

A Foundation Course for Language Teachers *by Tom McArthur*

Foreign and Second Language Learning – Language-acquisition research
and its implications for the classroom *by William Littlewood*

Communicative Methodology in Language Teaching – The roles of fluency
and accuracy *by Christopher Brumfit*

The Context of Language Teaching *by Jack C. Richards*

English for Science and Technology – A discourse approach
by Louis Trimble

Approaches and Methods in Language Teaching – A description and
analysis *by Jack C. Richards and Theodore S. Rodgers*

Images and Options in the Language Classroom *by Earl W. Stevick*

Culture Bound – Bridging the cultural gap in language teaching
edited by Joyce Merrill Valdes

Interactive Language Teaching *edited by Wilga M. Rivers*

Designing Tasks for the Communicative Classroom *by David Nunan*

Images and Options in the Language Classroom

Earl W. Stevick

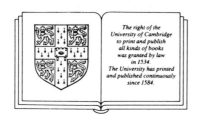

The right of the
University of Cambridge
to print and publish
all kinds of books
was granted by law
in 1534.
The University has printed
and published continuously
since 1584.

Cambridge University Press

Cambridge
New York   Port Chester
Melbourne   Sydney

Published by the Press Syndicate of the University of Cambridge
The Pitt Building, Trumpington Street, Cambridge CB2 1RP
40 West 20th Street, New York, NY 10011, USA
10 Stamford Road, Oakleigh, Melbourne 3166, Australia

First published 1986
Third printing 1989

Printed in the United States of America

Library of Congress Cataloging-in-Publication Data
Stevick, Earl W.
Images and options in the language classroom.
(Cambridge language teaching library)
Bibliography: p.
Includes index.
1. Language and languages – Study and teaching.
I. Title. II. Series.
P51.S853 1986   418'.007   85-14947

British Library Cataloguing-in-Publication Data
Stevick, Earl W.
Images and options in the language classroom –
(Cambridge language teaching library)
1. Language and languages – Study and teaching
I. Title
418'.007 P51

ISBN 0 521 32150 6 hardcover
ISBN 0 521 31281 7 paperback

The excerpts from Frederick Siedel's poem "Last Entries in Mayakovsky's Notebook"
on page 18 is reproduced with permission from *Sunrise,* by Frederick Seidel. ©
Frederick Seidel 1968. Reprinted by permission of Viking Penguin, Inc. and
Chatto & Windus, Ltd.

Contents

Preface

This book explores the relationship between the images in the mind of the learner and the options that are available to the teacher. My interest in imagery had its origin at the Anglo-American Center in Mullsjö, Sweden, in the summer of 1980, when the psychologist Berndt Brehmer challenged some of my ideas about perception and memory. In so doing, he started a chain of reading and thinking that is still continuing.

The "options" part of the title grew out of work in 1982, when I was trying to show some of my fellow volunteer English teachers the rich possibilities that they were overlooking in two sets of materials that we were using with Spanish-speaking beginners. Then I began to see that what I was learning about imagery could provide a principled basis for finding and for choosing among what I had been calling *technemes* (1959) or *informed choices* (1982) or *options*. That is what this book is about.

Images and Options is for new teachers and also for teachers who have spent many years at their work. It is for all teachers who are ready to take a fresh look at what their students are doing. Widdowson (1983:106) has observed that the most basic concepts of language learning are in fact principles that control all learning. In that sense this book is really about teaching anything at all, and not just English as a second language or French or Portuguese or Japanese.

This is primarily a book for teachers in the plural. It can of course be read by one person at a time, but it will yield more to groups of two or three teachers who work through it together step by step, first answering individually the questions that are asked, then comparing their answers and weighing one possibility against another.

It is customary in teacher-training manuals for the writer to set forth certain ideas at the beginning of a chapter, and then to suggest at the end of the chapter various questions for readers to discuss or activities for them to undertake. In this book I have reversed that order. The exercises come first, and ideas are developed out of experiences that can be expected to flow from the exercises. Moreover, most of the exercises invite or even require readers to draw on, and therefore to activate, the experiences that they themselves have had whether as teachers or as students. In both of these respects, I have tried to train teachers in a way consistent with how I hope they will teach their own students.

Preface

All of the exercises in Chapters 1–5, and much of what is in the remaining chapters, originated either in teacher-training courses and workshops or in ESL classes I have taught within the past five years, including several activities at the Foreign Service Institute. Students in classes at St. George's and Grace Episcopal churches in Northern Virginia provided the reality against which many of the specific techniques were tested, and Russell Ash through his helpful questions clarified my thinking about options. I would like to thank James E. Alatis, Dean of the School of Languages and Linguistics, and Walter A. Cook, S. J., Chairman of the Department of Linguistics, for allowing me to teach a methods course at Georgetown University; and especially I would like to thank my students in that course for their vigorous and helpful reactions to an earlier draft of this book.

Glossary

These definitions are intended as a convenience and summarize how I use these terms in this book. They are not presented as standard definitions.

communicative: An act, including a speech act or part of a speech act, on the part of one person is communicative to the extent that it changes something in the mind of another person. This definition is by no means original with me. I think, however, that people have sometimes concluded from it that a given sentence either is or is not communicative, rather than viewing communication as a matter of level and degree. I also think that the definition has often been applied in an overly narrow sense to refer only to changes in information about the external world or about internal states that the speaker consciously wishes to communicate through words.

flag: I have used this term for any word or short phrase that signals the purpose of an utterance or part of an utterance without giving information about the content. For example, use of the phrase "that may well be, ... " with a certain intonation indicates that the speaker is making a minimal concession in preparation for presenting a counterargument, yet it tells nothing about the subject of the disagreement.

image: This concept, which is central to the entire book, has been the subject of many and conflicting definitions in the literature. As used here, the term refers to the totality of reactions that one has to a given word or experience. These reactions are present in many dimensions, only one of which is the visual. An image in this sense may or may not include quasi-sensory perceptions of a visual or other nature. An image can influence behavior even when it is more or less incomplete. We have images of the spoken or written forms of words, as well as of physical objects and experiences.

item: This is a cover term for anything that the human nervous system can be shown to have held on to. Items exist in many dimensions beyond the traditional five senses. Larger and complex items are made up of smaller, less complex items. Any stored item presumably has some sort of neurochemical basis in the brain.

logogen: This term, borrowed from John Morton and others, refers to any network which provides the instructions for producing or recognizing the spoken or written form of a word or other linguistic unit. It may also be called a verbal image.

meaningful: A speech act is meaningful to the extent that its linguistic form is intended to be consistent with some reality which is outside of it and which does not depend on it. Like the definition of *communicative*, this definition is intended to be a conventional one.

network: This term has long been used in description of memory. A network is a set of nexuses which have interlocking relationships with one another. Such a network is not a static configuration, but is rather the basis for active generation of images. Networks contain and are contained by one another, and in a normal nervous system all networks are ultimately connected to one another.

nexus: The connection between two items that are associated with each other in memory. This connection presumably has its neurochemical side, which is almost certainly not as simple as a single neuron.

pattern: A pattern is a recurring relationship among relationships. For example, the semantic and formal relationship between *hill* and *hills* is the same as the semantic and formal relationship between *star* and *stars*. The meaning behind the phrasing of this definition is, I think, consistent with most people's use of the word *pattern*.

Part 1 Mostly about images

Learning a language (or anything else) is a matter of holding on to new words, new patterns, new skills, and new meanings. In this broad sense, learning depends on memory. Memory of course includes the sorts of thing that we call "memorization," in which a student works to be able to give back *Stadt* in response to *city*, or to recite a dialogue or a paradigm, but memorization is only one way – and a relatively unimportant way – in which new words, skills, patterns, and meanings get into memory and become available for future use.

The thesis of this book is that memory and availability depend on mental imagery, though I will be using that term in a way that is rather more specialized than the everyday sense. Because recent work on mental imagery has received relatively little attention within our profession, the first three chapters will develop some basic concepts in that field as they apply to *language* teaching. Chapter 1 consists mostly of activities which build some of the basic components of a concept of mental imagery and which therefore bear no direct resemblance to what we do in a language classroom. Chapters 2 and 3 are constructed around simulated dialogs and other exercises. In Part II (Chapters 4–8), we will apply these concepts to actual published classroom materials.

Each chapter consists of a series of exercises followed by comments. I suggest that before you read a comment you complete the exercise at least in your own mind, and preferably with someone else. If you start out knowing what your own experience and your own judgment tell you, you will be in a better position either to profit from or to differ with what I have to say! I also suggest that you do the exercises one at a time as they come, and not read ahead.

Several key words recur throughout this book. Because a few of them are used in ways that will be unfamiliar to most readers, a brief glossary has been provided at the front of the book.

1 Items, nexuses, networks, and images

Exercise 1.1

1. Listen once as someone reads the last few lines of a poem by Frederick Seidel on page 18. (If you are working alone, read the poem *aloud once* to yourself.)
2. Consider in your own mind the first of the following questions, and jot down a few notes for your own use. Then compare your answer to the answers of any other people who are working through this exercise with you. After brief discussion of differences or surprising similarities, go on and treat the remaining questions one at a time in the same way. You will get more value from the comments that follow the exercise if, before you look at them, you first bring your own resources to bear on the exercise itself.
   a. What pictures, if any, formed themselves in your mind as you listened to the poem?
   b. What color was the petal for you? What kind of flower or tree did it come from?
   c. Was the dancer a man, or a woman? How much of the dancer's body did you see? Was the dancer moving, or standing still?

COMMENTS

There are of course no right or wrong answers to any of these questions. Whenever I have done this exercise with groups of people, the replies have illustrated three points that are fundamental for the thesis of this book: (i) Words that have come into our heads from reading or listening commonly leave us with pictures, sounds, and feelings in our minds. (ii) In response to the same series of words, the pictures in the head of one person are commonly different from the pictures in the head of another person. (iii) The pictures that we form in response to words commonly contain some details which have no direct basis in the words themselves: the color of the petal, for example, or the sex of the dancer.

In using this exercise with hundreds of people, I have found that perhaps 1 person in 20 reports no visual pictures at all in response to hearing the poem, and that a few claim *never* to get mental visualization from purely verbal input. One person claimed to get pictures from words in her own native language, but not in a foreign language that she spoke very effectively.

Exercise 1.2

1. Without hearing or seeing the Seidel poem again, try to write it out verbatim. (To do so perfectly under these circumstances is an almost impossible task, but write down whatever words and word sequences you can. Take your time!)
2. Compare your fragments with those that others have come up with. Which words or word sequences were remembered by almost everyone? Which by only one person? Which "recalled" fragments do you now feel were spurious? Have you any guesses as to where the spurious fragments came from?
3. As a group, put together a composite reconstruction of the poem, drawing on anything that seems correct in any of the partial versions.
4. Now look at the poem as printed on page 18. Was the group effort that came out of step 3 more complete and more accurate than the versions produced by individuals in step 1? Which *ideas* were remembered by everyone? Which words or groups of words? Which ideas or words were remembered by no one or by only one person?

COMMENTS

This exercise has in the past dependably illustrated three additional points: (i) Once people have gotten a message out of a series of words, whether by reading or by hearing, they tend to hold on to the message but forget the exact words. (ii) Some parts of the message carried by a series of words are more likely to be retained than other parts. (iii) The words that are most likely to be retained are the ones most closely tied to the parts of the message that have been retained – in this case, the picture of the petal and the dancer.

Many other poems or pieces of prose could have been used to illustrate the points listed in the comments on these first two exercises. This poem, regrettably, uses *man* and *his* to mean all people regardless of gender. I have included it anyway because it catches so nicely the relationship between language and life: Our job is not so much to teach language (which will later be used by our students) as it is to teach people (who during and after our courses, for purposes of their own, will use language).

Exercise 1.3

1. Think of a word that you have learned recently, in your native language or in a foreign language.
2. Answer as many of these questions as you can about the experience of learning it:
   a. Did you learn the word by hearing it or by reading it?
   b. When did you learn it? At what time of day?
   c. Where were you? In what part of the room? Facing in which direction? Were you standing? Seated?
   d. What was the weather like? Were you comfortable?
   e. What other persons were with you? What (if any) was their role in your learning the word?
   f. How were you and the other person(s) dressed?
   g. How did you feel in general? How did you feel about learning the word?
   h. What was your purpose in learning it?

COMMENTS

People can generally answer most of these questions, and occasionally all of them. The important point here is simply that the range of associations which are connected with words as we learn and use them is quite broad.

Exercise 1.4

1. Overnight, take not more than ten minutes and try to memorize the Seidel poem at the end of this chapter so that you will be able to recite it at full speed, without errors and without hesitation.
2. At the next meeting of your working group, or on the following day if you are working alone, verify your ability (or inability) to recite the poem.
3. Answer each of the following questions to yourself, and then compare your answers with those of other people:
   a. On a scale of 1 to 10, how well would you say you performed?
   b. What was your emotional reaction to being required to memorize something?
   c. What did you do in order to memorize the poem?

COMMENTS

For a number of years, this sort of perfect memorization and fluent recitation applied to dialogs was considered by some to be the very basis of sound methodology in the teaching and learning of foreign languages. As you may have discovered while doing this exercise, a few people memorize easily and happily, for many memorization is a chore, and a few have strong emotional and even physical reactions against it. Furthermore, some of the people who have the strongest negative reactions to memorization are people who are quite good at picking up foreign languages.

People who do memorize vary greatly in how they go about it. Some read the text aloud a few times and then try to say it from memory, looking back at the printed version when necessary and continuing in this way until the process is complete. Others may begin at the beginning and gradually add lines until they reach the end, or they may begin at the end and work backward, or they may start with the part that is easiest to remember and build the remaining words in around that core. Some prefer to write the poem several times.

The points illustrated by this exercise are that, here again, people differ greatly in how they prefer to approach a simple task and that a type of activity may itself become the object of strong emotions, quite aside from its content.

Exercise 1.5

1. Listen to the list of words on page 18. (If you are working alone, read them *aloud once*, sliding your hand or a piece of paper down the page so that you can see only one word at a time.) The words should be timed about two seconds apart.
2. Count backward by threes from 371 until you have gone below 300. Count aloud and as rapidly as possible.
3. Write as many of the words as you can remember, in any order.
4. Without looking again at the original list, compare your list with those of others who are working with you. Which words were remembered by everyone? Which by no one or by only one person? What "recalled" words, if any, turned out to be spurious?
5. What did you hold on to most clearly as you stored and then recalled the words? Their sound? Visualized written or printed words? Something else?

COMMENTS

This exercise is an adaptation of a procedure which has been used in many laboratory experiments on human memory. The questions in step 4 have to do with what was recalled. If you are working with 20 or 30 other people instead of only two or three, go through the original list and see how many people recalled each word. Audiences with whom I have done this exercise generally have come out with results that are consistent with what research predicts: The first word or two are recalled by almost everyone, but the fate of the remaining eight is less certain. This result may be related to the fact that most of us also tend to remember best the first two or three people we meet in a large group, or that our students often recall the first consonant of a foreign word more dependably than they recall the later parts of the same word.

The questions in step 5 have to do with how things were stored and recalled. The most dramatic point illustrated here is again that there are very clear differences between people in how they approach a simple task like remembering a list of words. The people who have gotten all or almost all of the words in this exercise have reported various techniques. Some "read" the words from what they have "written" in their minds. Others hear the echo of the voice of the person who read the list aloud and so are able to write the words down as if from dictation. Many report that they formed mental pictures as the list was read, and that in recall they simply listed the names of the objects they could still see. One person reported that each of the words had created some sort of emotional response in her, and that when she was asked to write the words, she first recalled the series of feelings and asked herself what word had recently been associated with each. Another person said that what he recalled directly was a set of "life essences" which had come into his mind as the list was read, and that he had been able to retrieve the words using the "essences" as intermediaries.

Two other points are less dramatic but more basic: that a word can produce a wide range of pictorial, auditory, orthographic, visceral, and other items which have been associated with it in the past experiences of a particular hearer (as we saw in exercise 1.3) and that, although all hearers are presumably capable of having and remembering the full range of visual, auditory, emotional, and other sensations, each mind has its own favorite kind of data to which it refers most readily in routine tasks.

Exercise 1.6

1. Look for one minute at the list of Swahili words and their English equivalents on page 18.

2. Write out, in reverse chronological order, the names of as many of your secondary schoolteachers as you can remember in one minute.
3. Write out, as accurately as you can, the Swahili words for *conversation* and *crocodile.*
4. Write as many other Swahili words as you can recall.
5. If you are working with other people, compile a composite list of your written responses to step 3.
6. Using the results of step 5, try to reach a consensus on the correct answers in step 3. Then verify your results by looking again at the list of words. Was the consensus more correct than any of the individual responses had been, or less so?
7. Most important of all, list the *parts* of these words that anyone remembered correctly.

COMMENTS

In exercises 1.1 through 1.5, we were dealing with memories that appeared to be for "whole things": whole pictures, whole feelings, whole words, and so on. Either we got a particular word back or we did not. The most complicated thing that could happen was that we would mistakenly report *rock* when we had actually heard *stone* in exercise 1.5. In this exercise, however, we are dealing with alien words, which don't come back as nice wholes the way the English words did. In step 7, people typically find that they have held on to such fragments as "four syllables," "begins with *ma-*," "has two *m*'s," "has a *z* somewhere," "contains *-zungu-*," "has lots of u's," "has three u's," and so on. In fact, you may want to go back now to your data from step 3 and add to your answers to step 7!

In this book, we will say that each of the fragments listed in the preceding paragraph is a separate *item.*[1] An item in this sense is anything, large or small, that a human mind can be shown to have held on to. *Mazungumzo* may be an item, *ma-* may be an item, and the whole list of Swahili and English words may be still another item.

As we have seen in the earlier exercises, what is retained may be either verbal or nonverbal. We commonly think of verbal items as sentences or words or, at the very least, prefixes, suffixes, and stems; but vowels and consonants, and what linguists call the distinctive features of vowels and consonants, as well as rhythmic structure are also demonstrably verbal items. We may remember nonverbal items which are not sufficient

---

1 Recognizing that the terminology in this book is a bit special, I have provided a glossary at the front of the book. I've also pulled some of the principles together at the end of this chapter, and have given partial summaries at the ends of the chapters.

to bring back the whole meaning, for example, *magenta* is merely "some kind of red," or *Ed Walters* is just "somebody I knew in high school."

Similarly, we are accustomed to thinking of nonverbal items as consisting of objects, colors, acts, and other things for which we have words, but they are found in many dimensions other than these. It is also important to remember that emotions and purposes are items par excellence. Schank (1982: 92) in fact suggests that goals or purposes may be the basis of memory organization.

From "item" to "image"

In this book so far, you have met two lists of English words. If you were asked to recall any one of the words that occurred in the same list with *moon* or with *crocodile*, you could probably do so with few or no errors. That is, you would be unlikely to supply a word from the wrong list — *path* to go with *conversation*, for example. It is a well-known fact of memory that two items, once they have occurred together in the consciousness of an individual, may from then on have the property of bringing each other back to the consciousness of that same individual. This doesn't always happen, of course, but it often does. Two items that bring each other back in this way are tied to each other by something that we can call a *nexus*. A nexus in this sense presumably has some sort of neurochemical existence.

But just as items do not occur only two by two in life, so a nexus never occurs in isolation. In any real experience, every item has separate nexuses with many of the other items in that same experience, so that many, many nexuses are formed out of even a relatively simple experience. For example, the petal, the dancer's heel, and listening to a poem are three items from the experience of exercise 1.1. There is, at least potentially, a nexus between the petal and the heel, and between the heel and listening to a poem, and between listening to a poem and the petal. A person for whom all these nexuses are active may hear some other poem and be reminded of the petal, and from that be reminded of the dancer's heel. Or the same person may happen to see the petal of a flower and so be reminded of one or both of the other two items. We can use the word *network* to stand for such a set of interlocking nexuses that share a number of items. This term has been widely used in studies of memory for many years. Since a network is made up of nexuses, it too has some sort of neurochemical reality.

9

Exercise 1.7

If you are like most people, you think that you have more trouble than most other people in remembering personal names. Sometimes we think we have recalled a name, but it turns out to be wrong. For example, a colleague who heard me talking about a friend whose last name was Ash referred to the friend a few minutes later as "Mr. Bush." He had the right number of syllables, the correct last consonant, and he had even retained the fact that the name means a large plant. All he had wrong was the syllable onset and the vowel. So he was actually only 40% wrong and 60% right!

1. Working individually, jot down a few personal names that you can remember having trouble with. Next to each name, write the incorrect form(s) that occurred to you before you arrived at the correct form. Which items within the word did you get right first?
2. Compare notes with other members of your group.
3. What does this experience suggest with regard to the teaching of vocabulary?
4. If you want to have a little good, clean fun, here is something you can try with people outside your group. Casually use a personal name or a foreign word in the presence of an audience. Several minutes later ask each person to write his or her best recollection of the word or name, and then you write on the board the versions that people report. When I have done this, most people have come up with some complete word or name, but no one has remembered the name perfectly; but each person has retained his or her own set of authentic component items.

   If you are working with a dozen or more people, another way of exploring the same effect is to choose some surname that is well known but not very common. I once used *Simmons*. Make up sets of hints and put them on cards so that each card has three different hints. Some samples are:

two syllables
more than one syllable
stressed syllable rhymes with *him*
an English name
first consonant is *s*
contains more than one nasal consonant
no two syllables have the same vowel
name of a mattress company

Ask each group to come up with three surnames that are consistent with their three hints. Some groups may actually hit on *Simmons*, but that is not the point. The point is rather to illustrate the process by which we frequently recall a wrong name on the basis of a partial set of items, each of which has been derived from and is consistent with the original name.

COMMENTS

In this set of activities, we are able to observe a process which usually takes place so rapidly and so accurately that we don't notice it: (a) The mind holds on to some but not all of the items that are available from an experience such as hearing a name. (b) It then fills in the gaps by using items which in the past have been associated with the items that have been retained. (c) The resulting composite of authentic and added material becomes the basis for what we speak or write – or perceive! This composite, which results from the mental activity of (a)–(c), is an *image*, which *may or may not* lead to a percept-like visual experience. This concept of image will recur many times in the pages that follow.

The process of filling in gaps usually takes place so rapidly and so accurately that we can't notice it. When it is slow, however, or when it gives the wrong result, we can get a glimpse of how it works. Recently I was looking at the following words: "Their bones shall be scattered at the mouth of Sheol, like splinters of wood or stone on the ground. But my eyes are fixed on thee." I found myself looking for the word *axe* but not finding it. The verbal and nonverbal imagery that go with this word had apparently been put together consistent with the picture of the splinters on the ground, plus the occurrence of the relatively infrequent letter *x* in the following typographical line.

This sense of the word *image* differs in at least two ways from how the word is commonly used. (i) People often use it to mean something purely visual – something that they see or almost see in their mind's eye. As I am using the term, it includes not only what can be seen, but also what can be heard, felt, or otherwise experienced. (ii) People sometimes talk about storing images. I think that it is more realistic to think of what is stored as items (see comments on exercise 1.6), which are connected to one another by networks of nexuses. As I implied in the first part of this comment, an image is something that we perceive (more or less vividly, and in many more ways than merely visual) as a result of the interaction between what we have in storage and what is going on at the moment. Because this is a subtle distinction, it may seem unnecessary, but it is not. The main advantage in this view of imagery is that it accounts for the many distortions and partial errors which are important parts of language learning, as well as of everyday life. Another advantage is that it keeps us from having to postulate the separate storage of each of the uncountable scenes and impressions to which a person is exposed in the course of a lifetime.

In practice, then, getting a name wrong can be encouraging as well as discouraging, because frequently when we say we've gotten a name wrong, we've actually gotten it partly right. A teacher who cannot see what is right in a student's answer as well as what is wrong in it is half blind; a teacher who does not build on whatever correct elements the student has already retained is wasting time and energy.

Exercise 1.8

Most of the time, groups of items that have occurred together several times in the past form networks which operate smoothly, quickly, and dependably to give us consistent images. For example, the nonverbal items *used for writing, erasable, long and thin,* and the verbal items *two syllables, first syllable accented, first sound is p-, last sound is -l, contains an n somewhere,* and so on, work together to allow me to think immediately of the word when I see or need the object and to visualize the object if I hear or read the word. This is after all normal for one's native language. But there is one word for which, after quite a few decades of speaking English, something is wrong with my own personal set of networks. This involves the lower part of the human leg. When someone else uses the word *calf,* I have to stop and go through the following routine before I can interpret it:

a. *Calf* and *thigh* are the two parts of the leg.
b. The thigh of a chicken is the thicker, therefore the upper, part of a chicken's leg.
c. Therefore the thigh is the upper part of a human leg.
d. Therefore the calf is the lower part.

I have to go through the same routine when I want to use the word myself.

When I have told colleagues about this little glitch in the working of my English networks, they have sometimes replied with comparable stories of their own.

1. Devise a comparable routine for someone who cannot remember *foot* as a part of the human body.
2. Working individually and following the same routine, list three verbal and three nonverbal items in your network for *horse.* Then compare

your results with those of other group members. Which items were
mentioned by more than one person? Which by only one person?
3. Repeat step 2 for a culturally loaded word such as *justice*.
4. Find out whether anyone else in your group has noticed a comparable
gap in a native-language network.

COMMENTS

Although the four-step routine that I use for *calf* may sound like something from Rube Goldberg, it is not something that I consciously in-
vented. The alternate sequence of nexuses was there all the time. It would
be easy enough to find a good circuitous route for getting at the word
foot as a part of the human body, but I don't need that bit of help. It
just happens that my network for that word operates quickly and dependably, like 50 meters of superhighway. The 2-kilometer detour around
Robin Hood's barn is therefore unnecessary. A person takes such a
detour – resorts to indirect sequences of associations – only when the
direct connection is for some reason unavailable.

Exercise 1.9

I have a similar gap in my knowledge of German, a language which I
have been able to speak and read fairly effectively (at the Foreign Service
Institute's 2 level or better) for over 40 years. This gap has to do with
the pronunciation of the spellings -*ei*- and -*ie*-. When I see a familiar
word that contains one of these spellings, I have no trouble with it.
When I see one of them in a new word, however, I have to stop and go
through the routine:
a. The vowel sound is either that of English *see* or that of English *sigh*.
b. The definite article *die* has the vowel sound of English *see*.
c. This word has / does not have the spelling found in *die*.
d. Therefore this word is pronounced with the sound of *die* / is pronounced with the other sound.

1. What similar difficulties, if any, have you found in using languages
which are foreign to you?
2. How could you describe this process in terms of the commentary on
exercise 1.8?

COMMENTS

The data for exercises 1.8 and 1.9 are similar in that the user of the
language had a feeling of uncertainty. This feeling came about when the

networks produced two competing images: the upper and the lower half of the leg, or the vowel sounds of *see* and *sigh*. The two exercises are, however, different in one important way. To make the choice required in exercise 1.8, the language user resorted to *lexical knowledge* within the native language. In the present exercise, the user made the choice by consulting a very simple *rule* about the foreign language.

The choice is unnecessary for me in familiar German words because plenty of unambiguous resources are available to generate the needed word image. These resources include sound–letter nexuses other than those that involve *-ei-* or *-ie-*. They also include the meanings of nearby words, which among them suggest a short list of words, including the actual word, which could fit the context. Neither of these types of resource would be sufficient by itself.

Exercise 1.10

Spanish is a language in which I can communicate fairly effectively on simple matters, but which I have never studied and which I do not speak well. I had, however, formed a good linkage between the fairly frequent whole word *estuvo* (the third singular perfective form of the verb *estar* "to be") and the combination of meaningful items which go with it. On one occasion the meaningful items in a sentence I was trying to produce called for the third plural perfective form of the same verb, which doesn't occur quite so frequently as the singular. I traced the following steps in my own mental activity:

a. I knew that I had been exposed to the verb form that I needed here, but because I lacked a good linkage for this particular form, only the word *estuvo* came to mind.

b. *Estuvo* brought back a nonverbal item (singularity) which was not consistent with what I wanted to say.

c. The combination of nonverbal items next brought back the verbal image *estiveram*, which is the Portuguese equivalent of the Spanish form I needed. I was able to do this because I know Portuguese better than I know Spanish, and so I had a dependable linkage between the whole word and its nonverbal counterparts.

d. Nexuses based on past experience with pairs of Spanish and Portuguese words converted the final *-am* to *-on*, leaving me with *estuveron*.

e. This word was close enough to the actual Spanish form *estuvieron* so that it was able to bring that form back, and I recognized it as correct.

1. Have you had comparable experiences with languages that you know partially? Compare notes with the other members of your group.
2. In terms of exercises 1.8 and 1.9, describe the process by which a child learning English as a first language might come out with a form like *goed* (instead of *went*).

COMMENTS

This anecdote illustrates how the mind moves back and forth among size levels. Some of the items that figured in the process were relationships: basic verb meaning ↔ *est-*, for example. Others are relationships among relationships: The relationship between the final consonants of *bien* and *bem* (which mean "well") is *the same as* the relationship between the final consonants of *hablan* and *falam* (which mean "they speak"). A relationship is one kind of item, and the same is true of a relationship between relationships. A more common word for "relationship among relationships" is *pattern*.

The process of moving from the word *thigh* to an appropriate picture in exercise 1.8 involved the retrieval of nonverbal items, followed by the construction of a nonverbal image. The series of steps by which I arrived at the Spanish word *estuvieron*, on the other hand, involved the retrieval of verbal items followed by the construction of a verbal image. Some readers may find the phrase "*verbal* image" a bit surprising, since we normally use the word *image* in connection with pictures and other sensory experiences. I have chosen this terminology because what I will be calling *verbal images* are parallel to *nonverbal images* in at least four interesting respects: (i) Both are constructed from smaller fragments, which I have called *items*. (ii) Just as nonverbal items exist in many dimensions (sight, hearing, weight, time, purpose, emotion, etc.), so verbal items may in addition to their phonological features also include, among others, the vowel–consonant distinction, and part-of-speech membership, and memorized words and phrases, and unverbalized regularities, and verbalized rules. (iii) The construction of verbal images, like that of their nonverbal counterparts, takes place simultaneously along a number of parallel paths (see exercise 1.8). (iv) Just as our minds can derive verbal imagery from nonverbal stimuli, so they can also move in the opposite direction from words to pictures and sounds and feelings, and to countless other aspects of nonverbal experience.

Exercise 1.11

Here is a list of the main points that have been made in the comments for exercises 1.1–1.10. Study them in a way that will enable you to fill in the blanks in these sentences on a quiz. For example:

15

Mostly about images

Words that come into our .... from .... commonly leave us with
.... (including .... and ....) in our minds.

1. Words that have come into our heads from reading or listening commonly leave us with pictures (including sounds and feelings) in our minds.
2. In response to the same series of words, the pictures in the head of one person are commonly different from the pictures in the head of another person.
3. The pictures that we form in response to words commonly contain some details which have no direct basis in the words themselves.
4. Once people have gotten a message out of a series of words, whether by reading or by hearing, they tend to hold on to the message but forget the exact words.
5. Some parts of the message carried by a given series of words are more likely to be retained than other parts.
6. The words that are most likely to be retained are the ones most closely tied to the parts of the message that have been retained.
7. A word can produce a wide range of pictorial, auditory, orthographic, visceral, and other items which have been associated with it in the past experiences of a particular hearer.
8. People differ greatly in how they prefer to approach a simple task.
9. A type of activity may itself become the object of strong emotions.
10. Although all hearers are presumably capable of having and remembering the full range of visual, auditory, emotional, and other sensations, each mind has its own favorite kind of data to which it refers most readily in routine tasks.
11. An *item* is anything, large or small, that a human mind can be shown to have held on to. Items are verbal or nonverbal, and among the most important nonverbal items are emotions and purposes.
12. A *nexus* is the tie between two items that have the property of bringing each other back into the mind.
13. A *network* is a set of nexuses which share a number of items.
14. An *image* is a composite that we perceive (more or less vividly) as a result of the interaction between what we have in storage and what is going on at the moment.
15. An image includes not only what can be seen, but also what can be heard, felt, or otherwise experienced.
16. There is more than one chain of nexuses connecting any two items.
17. A person takes a detour – resorts to indirect sequences of nexuses – only when a more direct connection is for some reason unavailable.
18. A network may produce two or more competing images.

19. Faced by the need to choose between competing images, we some-
    times decide by consulting a simple rule about the foreign language.
20. A relationship between items is itself one kind of item, and the same
    is true of a relationship between relationships.
21. A more common word for "relationship among relationships" is
    pattern.

1. How did you go about preparing for a blank-filling quiz on these
   points? Was your study effective? Compare notes with others in your
   group.
2. How did you regard the requirement to study the points in this way?
   As a welcome recapitulation? As an annoyance? In some other way?
   Compare notes with colleagues.

COMMENTS

This list of points is intended to have two effects: It should bring back
some of the experiences, discussion, and thinking that were associated
with the individual exercises in this chapter. By placing the conceptual
statements next to one another, it should help readers to relate the
concepts to one another. The blank-filling task is easier if readers think
about the ideas behind the formulations; this thinking, rather than the
words themselves, is of course the purpose of the exercise. The first time
I used this exercise, I asked my class to try to reproduce the exact words
of the points. Synonyms were not to be sufficient. Reaction to this
requirement was sharply divided. A large number found that worrying
about the exact wording distracted their attention from the ideas. Others
said that it hadn't bothered them and that it may even have helped them
to assimilate the meanings. This difference among students may also be
important in the foreign-language classroom!

Texts for exercises

Poem fragment for exercise 1.1

> I know
> The power of words.
>
> It is nothing!
> A fallen
>
> Petal under
> A dancer's heel.
>
> But man
> In his soul, his lips, in his bones...

List of words for exercise 1.5

path
tree
moon
leaf
sword
stone
deed
pen
home
hand

List of Swahili words for exercise 1.6

nyumba	house
mazungumzo	conversation
mamba	crocodile
kitendo	deed
kalamu	pen
mazoezi	practice

In the literature

The fundamental concepts around which this chapter is built have grown from readings about memory and cognition, among them an article titled "Learning and Imagery" by B. R. Bugelski (1982), with extended commentary by many of his colleagues; John R. Anderson's 1984 "Spreading Activation"; Stephen Grossberg's article "A Theory of Human Memory" (1978); Vernon Hamilton's 1983 book *The Cognitive Structures and Processes of Human Motivation and Personality*; and J. D. Bransford's *Human Cognition* (1979).

Widdowson (1983: 6–7) has drawn a useful distinction between two kinds of purpose which he calls "aims" and "objectives," and has allowed us to forget neither that aims and objectives are different nor that in a successful program they must be consistent with each other. Items of purpose will be mentioned many times in the remainder of this book. They include both Widdowson's aims and his objectives, but they also include deep and more general purposes, such as "to make an impression," "to solve mysteries," or "to have fun." Perhaps a third term (*needs?*) should accompany *aims* and *objectives*. In this connection see Lacasa and Lacasa (1983) on student-perceived communication needs.

What Widdowson (1983: 34–5) and others have called "schemata" are approximately what in this book might be called "the networks that are responsible for high-level nonverbal imagery."

Morrison and Low (1983) provide a clear and useful treatment of an important application of the "parallel paths" concept.

The concept of image used in this chapter is confirmed most recently by Marks (1984: 96): "Images are in [a] special region of introspectively available data [for which] what is observed is always the product." He goes on to say, "Images are never free of associated emotions and thoughts and, like movements of the body, they are at the same moment both a stimulus and a response." Although for the purposes of writing about language study I have set up a two-way distinction between verbal and nonverbal, the latter is intended to include emotional and physical items as well as those derived from visual and other sensations. In this respect I agree with Ahsen (1984: 16) that "to experience [a nonverbal] image is not merely to inspect something on a display surface ... but also to experience a connective link with an interactive physiological field, namely the body."

An accessible discussion of how items of various kinds bring one another back (exercise 1.7) is found in Norman (1982: 41). On page 93 of the same book, Norman gives an interesting account of how magicians take advantage of this process in the minds of their audiences.

A students' text that clearly embodies many of the principles that recur throughout this book is *Listening Between the Lines* by Lin Lougheed (1985). It requires users to work with a great deal of nonverbal imagery which they have generated from the author's sparing and skillful use of words. The overall strategy of moving from individual creativity to work in small groups, and only from there to the author's comments, also parallels what I have tried to do here.

2 Imagery in work with fixed texts

Dialogs – or rather, one way of using dialogs – formed the basis of the Audiolingual Method. In that system, students first "mimicked" the words and the sentences of a "basic" dialog many, many times as the teacher carefully corrected their pronunciation. Then they were required to memorize the dialog well enough so that they could recite it fluently and correctly. Only when the dialog had been "overlearned" in this way did the class go on to other activities.

The Audiolingual Method has been out of favor during the past 15 or 20 years. It certainly had serious practical limitations, partly because it was based on a quite restricted idea of what happens in the process of language study. But dialogs can be used for other purposes than mimicry and memorization, as we shall see in this chapter.

The following dialog was obviously written not for real students, but for the in-service training of teachers. It had to be in a language that all users knew at least fairly well – therefore in English. At the same time, it needed to contain at least a few difficulties even for native speakers of English. That is the reason for the nonsense words, which some readers will recognize from Lewis Carroll's *Through the Looking Glass*.

Dialog J-1

1   A: Good afternoon! Mr. Lutwidge?
     B: Yes?
     A: Charlie Dodgson, from the American Embassy.
     B: Of course, Mr. Dodgson! Always nice to see you! Do sit down! What
5   can I do for you?
     A: Well, it seems we're to be visited by a member of the Congress.
     B: Yet another, eh? It never rains but it pours! And he'd like to visit the National Wabe, I suppose?
     A: She, actually. Her name is Alice Liddell. But yes, you're right, she'd
10   like to visit the Wabe. I think that's really what she's coming to Qalu Qallai for.
     B: Well, as you are aware, the Wabe is normally closed this time of year.

A: Yes, I know that. But Congresswoman Liddell is something of an
15   expert on raths. She's especially interested in mome raths, like the
   ones the Wabe is famous for.
B: I see. Well, I don't see why we can't work something out. I'm afraid
   she'll find our raths a little outgrabe, though.
A: I don't think so. She says they're the slithiest she's heard of.
20 B: How kind of her! Well, how about two o'clock next Wednesday?
   Would that suit?
A: Excellent! Thank you so much, Mr. Lutwidge! You've always been
   beamish to work with!
B: Don't mention it, Mr. Dodgson. Have a frabjous day!

Exercise 2.1

1. In what ways would this kind of dialog be suitable for use with
   intermediate students you have known? In what ways might it be
   unsuitable? Discuss your answers with members of your group.
2. In what senses can this dialog be called communicative?
3. In what senses can it be called noncommunicative?

COMMENTS

The word *communicative* is used in different ways by different people.
Dialog J-1 shows Lutwidge and Dodgson engaged in a lively and be-
lievable exchange of ideas. Students who produce the words of this
dialog, while at the same time generating in their own minds a series of
nonverbal images appropriate to the words, may in a sense be said to
be engaged in communication. This kind of communication contrasts
with the blind repetition of words and sentences like that done by one
student I observed, who was able to recite the sentences of a short dialog
easily, but who turned out to have matched the second foreign-language
sentence with the translation of the third sentence, and the third with
the fourth, and so on!

As other people use the term, however, an exchange of words is
communicative only when it causes some modification of the images in
the hearer's mind. The fictional Lutwidge and Dodgson may have been
altering the images in one another's fictional minds, but students who
reproduce their words are not altering meanings in one another's real
minds. Each student knows what the other student's next verbal output
is supposed to be, and each knows what his or her own next bit of
nonverbal imagery is supposed to include. From this point of view, no
prefabricated dialog can be communicative. That is a second sense of

"communication," and it is the one in which the term will be used throughout the rest of this book.

On another plane, however, even a prefabricated dialog is highly communicative in this second sense. Both teacher and student communicate not with *what* they say, for that is invariable. They communicate rather by variations in *how* they say it. In providing spoken models for students to imitate, the teacher may convey "This is fun," or "This is hard work and I am a taskmaster," or some other message. As students recite the dialog, they may show interest, or fatigue, or discouragement. Not least, the fluency and correctness with which students perform tells the teacher much about the degree to which they have mastered some of the mechanics of the language.

Several people who looked at dialog J-1 reported that the use of personal names for the speakers, rather than just A and B, helped them to form clearer visual images. One suggested, quite rightly, that the ability of such a dialog to generate images depends on how close it is to – or how far it is from – the general experience of the students: J-1 would create more pictures in the minds of university students, for example, than in the minds of people with little education and few contacts with world culture.

Exercise 2.2

Here is a series of questions in the target language, for discussion in the target language by a class of intermediate students.
1. In "Of course, Mr. Dodgson!" (line 4) the words *of course* mean:
    a. "Of course you may speak with me!"
    b. "I remember you very well!"
2. In line 6, the words *it seems* mean:
    a. "I think we're to be visited, but I'm not sure."
    b. "I'm a little reluctant to tell you..."
3. "Yet another, eh?" (line 7) suggests that:
    a. Lutwidge considers the number unacceptably high.
    b. Lutwidge is sympathetic with Dodgson.
4. "It never rains but it pours" (line 7) indicates that:
    a. Lutwidge is expressing sympathy.
    b. Lutwidge would prefer to talk about the weather.
5. In line 9, Dodgson uses the word *actually*:
    a. to confirm that it is true that Ms. Liddell would like to visit the Wabe.
    b. to show that he is giving some information that goes beyond what he had expected to talk about, or that he is making a tactful correction.

22

1. What would your own answers to these questions be? Do your answers agree with the answers of other people who are doing this exercise with you?
2. Which questions would probably be hardest for students of EFL/ESL?
3. What evidence can you find within the dialog to indicate that the correct answer to question 1 is (b)? What evidence can you bring from your own experiences in speaking English? Answer the same questions for question 3.
4. Write one or two additional forced-choice questions which will require the student to show understanding of the function of sentences in this dialog. (E.g., "Have a frabjous day!")

COMMENTS

Two of the forced-choice questions contain the verb *mean*. Nevertheless, they do not refer to dictionary meanings. All five of the questions are really about the purpose or purposes which the speaker of a sentence intended it to serve: to indicate recognition, to be courteous, to show reluctance, and so forth. The word *function* stands for this aspect of anything that is said or written. To put the same idea in another way, the *function* of a sentence is the purpose it serves in the ongoing inter-action – verbal and nonverbal – between people.

The function of a sentence has very little to do with its grammatical form. All three of the sentences:

Do sit down!

Won't you sit down?

I think you'll find this chair comfortable.

can serve the purpose of getting a visitor into a seat, even though the first is grammatically an imperative, the second is a question, and the third is a statement. In this sense they all have the same general function. Looking in the opposite direction, the function of a sentence is often impossible to guess without the help of context: "He's been beamish to work with" could be intended as a compliment to a father about his son, or as a factual report to a supervisor, or it could be spoken in the hope that the other person will come up with some informative comments or reactions. And of course the function of the sentence "Have a frabjous day!" is quite different from the function of "Have a hot biscuit!" even though they are identical in form.

The concept of function, then, is potentially quite valuable. Nevertheless, it can lead to some artificial problems. We can very easily and profitably talk about the communicative purpose (or purposes) of a particular sentence, but when we try to draw up a list, or a classification, of the functions in a language, we are likely to produce something which contains an embarrassing number of overlappings, omissions, and duplications. This is hardly surprising, for a list exists in one dimension, whereas what we are trying to put into that list is the full multidimensional range of human purposes.

Some people object that this so-called teaching of functions is in reality just the teaching of extra vocabulary, except that most of the vocabulary items consist of sentences or long phrases. This objection, however, overlooks the fact that more important than the actual verbal *items* taught (e.g., "Won't you sit down?") is the *focus* on communicative purpose in place of grammatical structure. We will take a more detailed look at the concept of function in Chapter 7.

Exercise 2.3

If the purpose of practicing a set dialog is to strengthen the ties between verbal and nonverbal images, then its effectiveness depends on the student's being able to generate the necessary nonverbal images while producing the words. Most of us professional language teachers are pretty good at generating such images in our own minds. Our students, however, vary greatly in this respect. We should not assume, as we listen to a student producing the words of a dialog, that the images going through the student's mind are comparable in richness and suitability to the ones that are going through ours. Here is a technique for increasing the likelihood that students will in fact generate adequate imagery to go with the words of a new dialog:

a. Students listen once, with books closed.
b. Students listen a second time, again with books closed, and ask questions about words that they do not recognize. Teacher replies. (Questions and replies are normally in the target language.)
c. Students listen a third time, following the dialog and its translation in their books.
d. During the fourth listening, students close their eyes and watch their own "home movies" as these are triggered by the words of the dialog.
e. The teacher goes through the dialog one line at a time, asking three different types of question about each line:
   – A *picture question*: "Was Lutwidge seated or standing when Dodgson walked in?" "Is there a rug in Lutwidge's office?" The answer to these questions must not be contained in or implied by the words of the dialog. There is no right or wrong answer, and each student will normally have a different one. Mutual amusement and incredulity often lead to excellent communicative practice here.
   – A *function question*: "In J-1, is Lutwidge expressing willingness to cooperate, or is he asking Dodgson to explain something?"

These questions and the students' answers are also in the target language. They are generally or-questions, because students at the intermediate level lack productive control of much of the vocabulary needed for the description of purposes or functions.

- *A rephrasing question*: "How else might Lutwidge have carried out his intent in line 17, where he says, 'I see.'?" Here, students must draw on their existing resources in the target language, focusing on both the meaning and the function of the sentence in order to preserve them in the paraphrase.

f. Once the dialog has been established both verbally and nonverbally in these ways, it can be used as the basis for any number of further activities.

1. Write question triads like those in step (e) for the first six turns in dialog J-1.
2. Exchange questions with the other people in your group. How did your answers to the picture questions you wrote compare with the answers of the others?

COMMENTS

Working through one triad of questions after another takes a bit of patience, but it seems to be worth it. At the end of a class session in which this technique was used, a student who had always been the slowest in his class was overheard to observe, "This is the first time, in any foreign language, that I've known what I was talking about." The formation of images takes time, and in a new language this time may be much longer than a teacher would expect it to be. The formation of images is also promoted when there is a definite occasion for forming them and when there is some kind of interesting outcome – some reward – for having formed them.

Exercise 2.4

1. Of the words *mome, slithy, outgrabe, beamish*, and *frabjous*, which are evidently favorable? Unfavorable? Neutral? What evidence should a student of English be able to find within the dialog which would help to answer these questions?
2. What part of speech do these five words belong to? On what evidence do you base your answer?
3. What is your own mental picture (if any) of a wabe? Could it be a postage stamp? A large animal? A social event? What pieces of information are there within the dialog which limit the possible meanings of this word?

COMMENTS

Our previous experiences with sentences like "How .... of ....!" (line 20 in dialog J-1) have led us to expect that the word in the first blank will be consistent with something in what has immediately preceded the sentence. Similarly, we know that with the possible exception of *slithy*, there is nothing in line 19 which would agree with *kind* as that word is used in line 20. One of the meaning items that has in many of our past experiences participated in nexuses with *kind* is *favorable*. We therefore infer that whatever *slithy* means, it must be (among other things) favorable.

Suppose now that in place of *slithiest* (line 19) the word *prettiest* had appeared. This is a familiar word, and many past experiences with it have linked it to (among other items) the idea of "favorable." In this case, the "favorable" item from *pretty* and the "favorable" item from line 20 agree with and reinforce each other. We normally take this sort of agreement for granted and don't even notice it. But suppose the word *stupidest* rather than *slithiest* had appeared in line 19. The nexuses in which this word has participated for most people do not include any ties with "favorable" or with other meaning items that fit with "kind." This lack of agreement immediately catches our attention, and we wonder whether someone has misspoken or we have misheard.

The relationship between *pretty* and *kind* in these two sentences is a simple example of the benign kind of *redundancy* without which everyday communication would be either impossible or insufferably time consuming.

Exercise 2.5

Many teachers like to ask their students questions about stories, dialogs, and the like. Here are two different types of question:

Type C:
a. What is Dodgson's first name?
b. Where does he work?
c. Who is coming to visit the embassy?

Type I:
d. How old is Lutwidge?
e. What does a wabe look like?
f. Do you think you would enjoy spending an hour with Alice Liddell? Why (not)?

1. Drawing on dialog J-1, write one or two additional questions of each type.
2. What are the advantages of each type of question? What are the disadvantages?

COMMENTS

We saw in exercise 2.1 that a sentence or any other act can be called communicative if it changes something in the mental imagery of a hearer or reader. A parallel term is *meaningful*. A sentence or other act is meaningful if it is chosen so as to be consistent with some set of facts outside of itself. Thus the sentence "The door is over there." is communicative if it carries new information to someone; if it states information that everyone already has about the classroom door or some other specific door, then it is not communicative, but it is still meaningful. If it is produced as part of a drill, then it is neither communicative nor meaningful, because it is governed not by facts but by the mechanical manipulation of words:

	The desk is over there.
blackboard	The blackboard is over there.
door	The door is over there.

In the lists of questions at the beginning of this exercise, the letter C stands for comprehension and the letter *I* stands for involvement, interpolation, and inference. Comprehension questions are a perennial favorite of language teachers all over the world. They have at least three advantages over inference questions: (i) They allow students to use many of the words and phrases of the original text, in a way which differs slightly from how they are used in the original text, but which is still meaningful in that the answers must remain consistent with the facts of the text. (ii) They require little or no vocabulary beyond what is contained in the text itself. (iii) They make minimal demands on the teacher's ingenuity or ability to improvise in the target language.

Comprehension questions also have at least two disadvantages: They are communicative only in the sense that the students' answers tell the teacher something about the students' understanding of the text and control of the language. They therefore tend to be perfunctory, and can easily slip from that to dull to tedious.

The advantages of interpolation questions are: (i) They are communicative, because not everyone can be expected to reach the same answer. (ii) They activate students' imaginations, thus enriching the nonverbal imagery which is tied to the verbal practice. (iii) They may provoke disagreement and discussion, and in that way broaden the range of purposes for which language is being used. (iv) They often lead to language which has some emotional content, again enriching the memory networks in which the words will participate.

The only real disadvantage of interpolation questions is that they place greater linguistic demands on students and teacher than comprehension question do. If students have too much trouble expressing their answers to inference questions, then it's best to stick with comprehension questions. If, on the other hand, a student's answer is incorrect but mainly clear and interesting, the teacher can just repeat it correctly, in a tone which indicates that the teacher is interested in it, or that he or she wants to be sure everyone else has heard.

Exercise 2.6

In exercise 2.5 we looked at a basic option that is available whenever we *ask questions* about a text – monolog or dialog – with which the students are familiar. The *answers* to those questions also carry with them some important options.

1. In your small group, come up with as many options as you can that relate to the grammatical form of the answers to comprehension or inference questions over a fixed text.
2. Write a few sample questions and answers, based on dialog J-1, which illustrate the options that you came up with in step 1.
3. What are some advantages and disadvantages of each choice?

COMMENTS

The option that language teachers are likely to think of first is whether students should be required to reply to the questions in complete sentences:

Who is coming to Qalu Qallai?
    Congresswoman Liddell is coming to Qalu Qallai.
    Congresswoman Liddell is.
    Congresswoman Liddell.

The advantage of the first of these alternatives is that students are able to draw on the wording of the question and so to have the experience of producing a complete sentence in the target language. A disadvantage is that it requires them to do something that is avoided in English and in any other language that I know anything about. To reply to a question with all of the words that it contained is usually a sign of irritation or sarcasm or condescension.

The advantages of the second alternative are that it is more idiomatic and that it does not convey undesirable emotional implications. The disadvantage is that if students are to produce their answers from explicit grammatical rules, then they must know the English rule that allows them in this context to reply "Congresswoman Liddell" or "Ccngress-woman Liddell is," but not "Congresswoman Liddell is coming." If, on the other hand, students are guided in making a few replies of this kind, they will have the experience of using such replies in situations where they belong. In so doing, they may pick up this simple trick without having to think about the rule, and thus may be able to use it later on without recourse to the rule.

But there is another alternative for the form of the answer. Each of the three variants given above is mechanically derivable from the question plus some bit of information. They are the staple fare of language study, something like meat and potatoes in a traditional American meal. It is also possible to add a sprig of parsley, or a bit of salad:

If I'm not mistaken, her name's Alice Liddell.
It's some American official. I think her name's Little, or something like that.
Hadn't you heard? It's the famous Alice Liddell!

In these examples, the sprigs of parsley are "If I'm not mistaken...," "It's some...," "I think...," and "Hadn't you heard?" A better term for little phrases like these might be *flags*, because they notify the hearer about how the rest of the sentence is intended to fit into the conversation. They do not, however, give any indication of the subject of the conversation: "If I'm not mistaken" or "Hadn't you heard?" could as easily be used in questions about the annual schedule of the National Wabe, or about a recent football match, or about anything else.

Giving answers that are garnished with this kind of parsley, or that carry flags like these, is a bit tricky. It may be a good idea for the teacher to take the role of answerer first, with the students asking the questions. In this way the students can get the feel of this kind of discourse, and at the same time they can pick up a few flags that they will be able to use later on.

Exercise 2.7

Here is dialog J-2. The characters, the setting, and the overall purposes are the same as those in J-1.

Dialog J-2

A: Good afternoon. Are you Mr. Lutwidge?
B: Yes, I am. Please sit down.

Mostly about images

A: My name is Charles Dodgson. I'm from the American Embassy.

B: How do you do, Mr. Dodgson? What can I do for you?

A: A congresswoman is going to visit the embassy here in Qalu Qallai. She would like to visit the National Wabe.

B: The Wabe is open during the months of May through September, but it will be closed beginning October 1. When does the congresswoman expect to arrive?

A: On September 30. But she will arrive in the middle of the day, and she will probably be tired. Could she visit the Wabe the following day?

B: Perhaps. Although the Wabe will be officially closed, the staff will still be there for a few days. They will be getting things ready for the winter.

A: That's good. Since they are going to be there for a few days, could the congresswoman visit the Wabe on October 8? She should spend the first week at the embassy if she can.

B: We will be glad to extend courtesy to a congresswoman. What is the congresswoman's name?

A: Alice Liddell.

B: Does that end with one *l*, or with two?

A: It ends with two *l*'s.

B: (*writing*) It's all arranged.

A: Thank you. Goodbye.

1. Compare this dialog with J-1. Look at linguistic difficulty, but also at the appropriateness of what is said, and at the degree of naturalness, and at any difference in the amount of imagery that the two dialogs produce.

2. Discuss these points with the others in your group. List examples of greater or lesser difficulty, appropriateness, and degree of naturalness, as well as examples of differences in imagery.

COMMENTS

Traditionally, students of a foreign language have been expected to produce correctly virtually all grammatical structures to which they have been exposed. Put the other way, this has meant that teachers and textbook writers have shied away from including in their materials more grammar than they think their students will be able to control. Since any departure from the most common patterns of the language has its own rules, and since learning and following each new rule is more or less of a burden on students, teachers and writers have tended to stick to the most basic structures.

The most basic sentence structure of English is Subject + (affirmative or negative) Verb Phrase + Something Else. The two most important changes to the basic sentence structure are in the formation of questions and subordinate clauses. Within the sentence, the most common noun phrase contains some sort of noun, and the most common verb phrase contains a main verb. These facts have been recognized instinctively by generations of language teachers, whatever their system for describing and labeling grammatical categories and relationships. For want of a better term, let's call this set of categories and relationships Intuitively Safe Grammar (ISG).

Exercise 2.8

Look at dialogs J-1 and J-2 from the point of view of the comment following exercise 2.7. Although neither J-1 nor J-2 was written with Intuitively Safe Grammar in mind, J-2 remains almost entirely within ISG, while J-1 departs from it at several points. This accounts for some of the comparatively wooden tone which you may have noticed in J-2 as you worked through exercise 2.7.

1. List the places in J-1 and J-2 at which the writer goes beyond Intuitively Safe Grammar.
2. In what other respects does J-2 seem more wooden, or less natural, than J-1?
3. Reach the best consensus you can on the following questions which might be asked by students:
   a. What is the difference between saying:
      Mr. Lutwidge?
      Are you Mr. Lutwidge?
      Pardon me, sir. Are you by chance Mr. Lutwidge?
   b. What is the difference between:
      Well, as you are aware, the Wabe is . . .
      You know that the Wabe is . . .
      The Wabe is . . .
   c. What is the difference between:
      Do sit down!
      Sit down!
      Have a seat!

COMMENTS

Each of the preceding alternatives can be expected to have a slightly different effect on the hearer. The choice of one or another of these effects is one part of the purpose of the speaker. It is thus one component

31

of the function of the sentence, just as the desire to verify the other person's identity, or to remind the other person of a fact, or to see the guest seated is a component of its function. The factors which make one of these alternatives more appropriate than others are determined by the total context. This is one reason for having students work with idiomatic and fairly long dialogs, in a context which is as fully developed as possible.

Native speakers may not agree entirely on just how to describe the differences among the above alternatives, and so the corresponding functional components may be difficult to label. As I remarked in exercise 2.2, published lists of functions tend to look ad hoc and a little fuzzy, with some items in the list appearing to be subcategories or partial duplications of other items in the same list, and with a number of evident omissions. Grammatical points, on the other hand, are relatively easy to identify. That may be one reason language teachers and writers of textbooks have generally tended to give prominence to the lists of prefixes and suffixes and grammatical structures that they cover, and to treat functions only incidentally. This fact does not make functions any less important for those who want to use a new language effectively.

Exercise 2.9

1. With which of the following two positions do you agree more closely?

Position A
The language in J-1 could almost be a transcript of something that had been said by two native speakers. The language of J-2, on the other hand, is very stiff and artificial. There is no real value in teaching students the language of J-2; it only misleads them about how the language is actually used, and it may even interfere with their ability to understand actual conversations later on. In addition to being misleading, it produces a dull, pedestrian tone to which even low-intermediate students are likely to respond unfavorably. Too many of the textbooks in use in the world today are written in this J-2 style. Although the grammatical rules behind J-1 are admittedly more complex than the ones behind J-2, they are not really all that difficult to *acquire* (as contrasted with *learn*), and early exposure in an intelligible context is the best way to acquire them.

Position B
Although it is true that J-1 is more idiomatic, it is also much harder for intermediate students to understand. More serious, such students will be much less able to use J-1 as a basis for their own new utterances, since its structure is based on rules which are more numerous

and more complex than in J-2. If students learn to speak like J-2, they may not sound perfectly native, but they will be understood, and will thus be able to sustain contacts with native speakers. If they have enough of this contact, they will acquire the necessary J-1 rules without formal instruction. If they do not have contact with native speakers, they will not need the J-1 style anyway.

2. Alone or in collaboration with a few other teachers, draw up your own statement on the relative merits of teaching students the kind of language in J-1 or J-2.

COMMENTS

The issue represented by these two positions was the subject of a long and very animated discussion in one of my classes. Gaining command of a language by exposure to it in fully meaningful and communicative contexts, without reference to explicit rules, is frequently called *acquisition*. Children necessarily "acquire" their first language, but under the right circumstances even adolescents and adults can pick up an amazing amount in this way.

Exercise 2.10

Here are two ways of introducing a dialog.

Technique D-1 (typical audiolingual)

a. The teacher reads the dialog all the way through. Students listen with their books closed.
b. The teacher reads the dialog a second time, pausing after each sentence. Students ask questions about anything they do not understand. The teacher answers each question briefly.
c. The teacher reads the sentences one at a time, and the students repeat in chorus. If a sentence is long, the teacher reads the last part, the students repeat, the teacher reads the same part plus what precedes it, the students repeat. In this way, the teacher builds up to the whole sentence.
d. This step is like (c), except that the students respond individually.
e. Students open their books and repeat the sentences aloud in chorus after the teacher.
f. The teacher reads one side of the dialog; individual students read the other. This process is repeated until students are able to respond without looking at the book.
g. As homework, students are assigned to memorize the dialog so that

they can repeat it without hesitation and without errors. This is often done with the help of an audiotape.

h. At the next session of the class, students act out the dialog with one another, using appropriate gestures and voice inflections.

i. The teacher suggests a situation similar but not identical to the one in the dialog. Students act this out, making appropriate changes.

Technique D-2

a. The teacher sets the stage: "N is going to take the part of an officer in an embassy. An important government official is coming to town, and this official would like to visit the mint. M is going to be the public relations officer of the mint. There may be some difficulties in arranging the visit."

b. The teacher asks students to suggest things that N and M might say to each other, and how they might say them.

c. N goes through the interview, with the teacher acting as the public relations officer of the mint.

d. M goes through the interview, with the teacher taking the part of the officer from the embassy.

e. Students listen to dialog J-1 or J-2 twice with books closed, then ask questions to clarify meanings.

f. Students listen again with books open, and again ask questions to clarify meanings.

g. Students listen again with books open.

h. Individual students read aloud words or short phrases which they have chosen from the dialog. The teacher repeats the words or phrases correctly, but with no overt correction of students' pronunciation.

i. Students listen again with books closed, watching their own "mental movies," as in exercise 2.3.

j. The class observes 90–120 seconds of silence.

1. Working as a group, devise a third technique for presenting a dialog like J-1.
2. How does each of these three techniques manage mental imagery?
3. What are the advantages and disadvantages of each?

COMMENTS

The most obvious difference between techniques D-1 and D-2 is that the former concentrates first and primarily on verbal imagery, while the second begins by mobilizing and developing relevant nonverbal imagery through use of familiar language. The use of silence in technique D-2 (step j) has proved empirically useful, perhaps because it allows the brain time for physiological processing of the new nexuses between verbal and nonverbal material.

Summary

Chapter 1 developed a few basic concepts on the nature of mental imagery. In Chapter 2, we have begun to look at some of the pedagogical applications of those concepts.

The term *communicative* is reserved for activities – verbal or otherwise – which modify the images in someone else's mind, and communication in this sense takes place through style and through tone of voice as well as through words. The word *function* refers to any and all of the purposes that are served by any given verbal or nonverbal act. Practice of words and sentences is effective only insofar as it takes place concurrently with the presence of appropriate nonverbal imagery, including items that represent purposes.

The formation of verbal images, and of the nonverbal images to accompany them, takes time – frequently more time than the teacher imagines it will. The systematic use of silence contributes to the formation of imagery, partly because it allows for time that is free of new input. The formation of images is promoted when there is a definite occasion for forming them and when there is some kind of interesting outcome – some reward – for having formed them. When the expectations and the imagery generated from one part of an act are consistent with the expectations and imagery generated from other parts of the same act, the result is a desirable and even necessary kind of redundancy.

A sentence or an act is *meaningful* if it is chosen to be consistent with some set of facts outside of itself. Certain words or groups of words, called *flags*, tell nothing about the content of a message, but indicate how a sentence or other part of discourse is supposed to fit in with other parts of the same act of discourse.

The term *Intuitively Safe Grammar* stands for a rather small set of grammatical categories and relationships to which teachers and textbook writers often revert when they are trying to make their language accessible to people who don't know much of it.

In the literature

An extensive list of functions (exercise 2.2) for low-intermediate English is found in J. A. van Ek, *The Threshold Level for Modern Language Learning in Schools* (1977).

Harmer (1982) discusses the question "What is communicative?" and Ellis (1982) treats informal and formal approaches to communicative language teaching. Paulston and Bruder (1975) explore the continuum that lies between manipulative and communicative activities.

Whitaker (1983) has some interesting things to say about comprehension questions. For further options in the asking of questions (exercise 2.5), see Stevick, *Teaching and Learning Languages* (1982), Chapter 12. Stephen Krashen has done more than any other one person to bring to the attention of language teachers the possibility that students may acquire language as well as learn it (exercise 2.9). A relatively recent treatment of this line of thinking is found in *The Natural Approach* (1983), written by Krashen and Tracy Terrell.

3 Imagery and the study of grammar

In Chapter 2 we looked at one very common element in language lessons, the prefabricated dialog. We tried our hand at revising and writing dialogs, and looked at a few of the options that are available to us when we use them. There was a time when some teachers thought that people could make the words and the grammatical structures of a new language their own by doing little beyond memorizing dialogs. That may in fact be true for those who can both hold on to the verbal images and at the same time generate from the words a fairly full set of nonverbal images, but most learners need other kinds of activity instead of or in addition to these. In this chapter, we will examine some ways of dealing more directly with points of grammar.

When students have difficulty in producing sentences that are grammatically correct, their instinct is to ask the teacher to explain it to them, and the response of the teacher often consists of an attempt at explanation. Explanation is only one way of trying to help students with grammatical questions, and it is very seldom adequate by itself. Nevertheless it is the most ancient and widespread way, so we'll look at it first. Because the use of articles in English gives some degree of trouble to speakers of all other languages, we'll take our examples from that area.

The conditions which govern an English speaker's choice to use one or another of the articles, or to use no article at all, are so complex that no simple, comprehensive, and airtight explanation is possible. Nevertheless, partial explanations can be helpful.

Grammar explanation A
(based on an actual note prepared by a real teacher of a language other than English, for real students)

English has two articles, called the definite article (*the*) and the indefinite article. The definite article is used when the noun refers to some specific person or thing. The indefinite article is used in referring to one person or thing which has not yet been mentioned in the conversation. Under some circumstances the article is omitted altogether.

Do you know *the* time?
Do you have *a* watch?

What is *the* matter?
I feel like eating *a* good steak!
Do you like steak?
He is *the* president of his club.
(Note that the indefinite article has the spelling *an* before vowels.)

Exercise 3.1

1. Working individually and then as a small group, list the ways in which explanation A might be helpful or unhelpful to someone learning English.
2. What *qualities* should one look for (or try to include) in a grammar explanation on any topic?

COMMENTS

Here are a few of the defects in explanation A: The form of the definite article is mentioned, but the form of the indefinite article is not. Aside from the information which was omitted, this lack of parallelism is a sign that the writer was not forming in his or her own mind a set of images of what the explanation might produce in readers' minds. Instead, the writer was setting down his or her own thoughts as they came to mind.

The information that is finally given about the form of the indefinite article is stated in terms of spelling, as though pronunciation were not involved. There is also no mention of the different pronunciations of *the* before vowels and consonants.

Maybe it's just a personal reaction of mine, but it seems to me that the only reason for writing a grammar explanation in the first place is to help readers to notice something that they might have overlooked. To begin an explanation with the words "Note (or notice) that . . ." seems to me under these circumstances to be redundant, tiresome, and pedantic.

The ultimate purpose of an explanation like this one is to help students to make future choices accurately, yet the examples given here do not show one of the articles in contrast with the other or with absence of any article. The last example, in fact, would be just as correct, and mean about the same, if the article were omitted.

The next-to-last example brings in a mass noun, with no indication of the effect that this has on the omission of articles. The explanation refers vaguely to "some circumstances."

Perhaps most grievous, the explanation gives no indication of its own incompleteness on a subject which is so very complex.

Grammar explanation B

An English noun may be accompanied by a possessive (*my, your,* etc.) or by a demonstrative (*this, that,* etc.). These words usually have fairly clear translations in other languages. A noun may also be accompanied by an article. English articles, however, lack clear equivalents in most other languages, and for that reason they can be difficult for many learners.

Articles in English are either definite (*the*) or indefinite (*a* before consonant sounds, *an* before vowel sounds). No simple rule can tell you exactly when to choose one of these articles or the other, or to omit the articles altogether. In general, however, English speakers use *the* when they think that the hearer or reader already has reason to know which person or thing they are talking about:

The pen in your pocket is leaking. (Assuming that the hearer has only one pen in his or her pocket.)
The moon is rising. (The earth has only one moon.)
Shall I open *the* door? (If there is only one door in the room.)
She is *the* president of the union. (An organization can have only one president at a time.)

If English speakers feel that the person or thing is not clearly specified in the mind of the hearer, they will use the indefinite article:

I bought *a* new pen. (We don't know anything else about the pen.)
A moon is rising. (Said on Saturn.)
Shall I open *a* window? (If there is more than one window in the room.)
He is *a* member of the union. (An organization can have many members at one time.)

Exercise 3.2

1. Working individually and then as a small group, list the ways in which explanation B might be helpful, or unhelpful, to someone learning English. How does it compare with explanation A?
2. Write an explanation of one page or less on the English articles, or on some other point in any language. Get the other members of your group to look it over and offer their suggestions.

COMMENTS

As we saw in exercise 3.1, the ultimate purpose of any grammar explanation is to help students to make choices more correctly and more quickly in their future use of the language. An explanation should therefore include three kinds of information: (i) What are the grammatical elements among which a speaker must choose? These elements may be of many kinds: inflectional endings, prepositions, intonation patterns, differing orders for the same set of words, and so on. (ii) What are the audible and visible forms of these elements? (iii) What are the criteria for choosing one element or another?

Here are some points to keep in mind when you write or revise (or evaluate) explanations of grammar:

a. Does this explanation make clear exactly what the choices are that it is supposed to help its readers to make?
b. Are the spoken and written forms clear?
c. Are the examples good, idiomatic phrases or sentences in the target language?
d. Do the examples actually illustrate the point that is being explained?
e. Are the examples drawn from meaningful contexts that have already been established in dialogs or elsewhere, or do they in some other way make it easy for students to form nonverbal images which will be appropriate to the words that they contain?
f. Are the criteria for choosing between *a* and *the*, or between *ser* and *estar*, or between the perfective and the imperfective aspect or whatever, stated in terms which can be used by readers who do not already make the right choices by instinct anyway?
g. Does the explanation make one point clearly and then stop, or does it ramble?

3. Answer these questions for explanations A and B, and for the explanation that you wrote in step 2.

Answering questions about grammar

When students become aware that a speaker of the target language has used a form in a way that they would not have predicted, they often become uneasy. At such times, they quite naturally ask questions. These questions usually begin with *why*.

Exercise 3.3

Here are some questions based on dialog J-1 (see beginning of Chapter 2), with two answers for each of the first two questions:

a. Why did he say, "Charlie Dodgson..." instead of "I am Charlie Dodgson"?
   – He could have answered "I am Charlie Dodgson," but what he

said made it sound as though he did not think he was particularly important.
- The subject and the verb *be* may be omitted if there is no danger of misunderstanding. In this case, since Dodgson was the only person in the room besides Lutwidge, there was no need to say, "I am..."

b. Why did Lutwidge say, "Do sit down" instead of "Sit down"?
- The use of the auxiliary verb *do* is the emphatic form of the verb phrase in the present tense. You can also use *did* with the past tense, but that would not apply to the imperative. The imperative uses only the present form.
- "Do sit down" carries more emotion, and more apparent concern for Dodgson's comfort. "Sit down" might have sounded a bit abrupt and impersonal.

c. Why did Dodgson say "like the ones the Wabe is famous for" instead of "the ones for which the Wabe is famous"?

d. Why did Dodgson say, "She says they're the slithiest she's heard of" instead of "She says they are the slithiest of which she has heard"?

e. Why did Dodgson say *"something of* an expert"?

1. What are the strong and weak points of each alternative in (a) and (b)?
2. Devise your own answers to questions (c)–(e).
3. What other questions might learners of English ask about the language in dialogs J-1 and J-2? How might you answer them?

COMMENTS

A good oral answer to a question about grammar should give the same kinds of information as a written explanation (exercise 3.2). There are two other points to keep in mind.

i. Any question represents a gap in the questioner's mental imagery about some matter. Although questions about grammar often begin with *Why?*, what the student really wants to know is *"When* should I use this form?" or *"How* can I tell which to choose?" If you restate the student's question in these terms, either aloud to the student or at least in your own mind, you are more likely to come up with a useful answer. Restating the question aloud also allows you and the student to be sure that you have accurately perceived the gap that the student wants to have filled.

ii. Oral answers should be brief: 5 seconds, or 10 seconds at the most. If you go beyond this, you risk losing the student as you go on and explore *your own* mental imagery about grammatical relationships and the like. Staying within these time limits allows you to give the student something that will fit into the gap in his or her mental imagery of the grammatical structure of the language. This something occasionally fills the gap completely, and the student is satisfied. Frequently it fills the gap only partially, leaving a new and smaller gap. When this happens, the student can ask a new question, and you can give another 5–10 seconds of answer.

Drills

Explanation is the most common way in which language teachers over the centuries have attempted to give students direct help with grammar. The mental imagery which is affected by explanations consists of verbal abstractions about the verbal side of the language – words about words. Some students are able to connect imagery on this level with the imagery which directly underlies their actual use of the language. These students get some benefit from explanations.

Another way of working on grammar is through the use of drills. Recent emphases on cognition, comprehension, and communication have led many practitioners to conclude that drilling has little or no place in enlightened language teaching. Perhaps they are right. Certainly drilling has been much overdone in some methods. Nevertheless, a future language teacher looking back at her own years as a learner reports:

What made an even greater impression upon me were her techniques of teaching grammar, specifically the dative and accusative prepositions and those infamous article and adjective endings. Her technique was based on drilling and memorization, both of which are often criticized. Her energetic style and persistence, however, made this an enjoyable way of learning. The charts and lists drilled into my head were most definitely of practical usage during my past year in Germany ... For these points to have stuck with me for the past 8 years, there's something positive to be said for the daily drilling and memorization of Mrs. V——'s eighth grade German class.

I cannot say that this student was typical of all students, and I will not say that methods should be constructed as though she were. On the other hand, I doubt that this kind of student is as rare as some people seem to think, and I suspect that there's at least a little of this kind of reaction in a large number of students.

Exercise 3.4

Here is a drill that is derived from the Lutwidge-Dodgson dialogs.

Drill E

Use *a* with each of the following words:

congresswoman   chauffeur
congressman   senator
reporter

1. How does the effect of this drill differ from the effect of a simple explanation of the use of the two forms of the indefinite article?
2. What are the strong and weak points of this particular drill?
3. What does this drill do with the mental images of the students?

COMMENTS

I can't remember ever running across a drill that was quite so primitive as this one, though I have seen a few that came close. Its structure has been simplified for purposes of discussion of the mental imagery involved. This drill rests on at least three assumptions: (i) The students already have available to them the combination of verbal items which dependably produce the word forms *congresswoman*, and so on. Borrowing a term from Morton (1969; Morton and Patterson 1980) and Warren (1972, 1974), I will call small networks such as these *logogens*. Logogens produce the images which are the direct basis for production of words or grammatical patterns. (ii) According to almost all methods, students also have available in their experience some kind of nonverbal imagery which corresponds to the meanings of these words. (iii) They have available at least some of the items of grammatical patterning which correspond to "noun-ness": use as subject of a verb, object of a preposition, and so on. (See Stevick 1982: 197 for a similar discussion.)

If the drill is to succeed, students must (iv) retrieve with each word some nonverbal imagery corresponding to its meaning and/or translation; (v) retrieve, along with the meaning, the items that represent its "noun-ness"; and (vi) experience the juxtaposition of the article *a* with successive occurrences of the "noun-ness" items. Once they have done these three things, they form and strengthen a nexus between *a* and "noun-ness."

To say the same thing in everyday language, students come away from this drill with a little more of a feeling that an English noun may be preceded by *a* and also that *a* is sometimes used before (but not after) nouns. This awareness that *a* and nouns sometimes go together is not nothing, particularly for students whose languages lack articles altogether. Nevertheless it falls far short of full knowledge about when to choose the indefinite article instead of the definite article or no article

43

at all. It falls even farther short of the skill to make those choices without effort and without thinking about them.

In the terminology that we developed in Chapter 1, the linguistic material that is stored as a result of a drill like E consists of a set of verbal images: short phrases, in this case. Any learner who can draw on a stock of verbal images has one way in which to arrive at a correct decision between *a* and *an* as the form of the indefinite article before a particular word: A student who wants to use any of the five nouns in drill E can go back and see/hear in his or her mind an instance in which a form of the indefinite article had already occurred before that same word.

Exercise 3.5

Here is a second drill on the indefinite article.

Drill F

Write *a* or *an* in each of the following blanks:

....	car	....	excursion
....	plane	....	umbrella
....	airplane	....	ticket
....	bus	....	opinion

1. How does drill F differ from drill E in the observable things that the student does?
2. How do the two drills differ with regard to mental imagery?
3. Which of the eight words in the drill does not fit with the rest?

COMMENTS

There are two obvious differences in what students do with the two drills: Drill E is to be done orally, while F requires students to write. In drill E, students always produce the same form, while in F they sometimes produce *a* and at other times *an*.

The *verbal* images of the eight words in drill F contain many items: first sound, first letter, number of syllables, number of letters, stressed vowel, last sound, and so on. In making the choice between *a* and *an*, the student must pay attention to only one of these items: the first sound. Success in the drill both requires and rewards this particular focus of attention when a word follows the indefinite article. This nexus is stored along with the feeling of success.

There is another aspect of imagery in these simple drills that deserves attention. All of the words in E stand for people who either are news-makers or are frequently around newsmakers. The first seven words in F stand for things associated in one way or another with travel. Each of the drills therefore has its own kind of cohesiveness with regard to the *nonverbal* imagery that it arouses. I suspect that this kind of thematic cohesiveness is helpful to students, especially the weaker ones. In drill F, the abstract noun *opinion* produces much less in the way of nonverbal imagery and is not associated with a clear topic such as "public affairs" or "travel."

There is a subtle but very important difference between drills E and F. The linguistic material in F includes the same kinds of verbal images as in E, but it also includes a recurring *relationship among* these verbal images – a relationship which hinges on one feature of the word that follows the article. These sentences therefore exemplify a very simple *pattern*. In deciding which form of the article to use, the learner who has a feel for this pattern has available a source which was not available to the learner who had only done drill E: The learner can respond to the relevant feature of the word, whether that word is a new one or one that he or she has already encountered. (These two paths sometimes conflict. Recently I heard myself say that something "had slidden" – presumably patterned after "had ridden." A split second later, the form "had slid" came to me, apparently from earlier verbal imagery that was triggered by certain components of the meanings that I was trying to express. I compared the two and decided in favor of the latter.)

There are some larger, and for that reason less noticeable, kinds of items which are also stored along with the experience of doing a drill. One is the consciousness of speaking English and not some other language: If the same student who has done this drill then switches to German, he or she is unlikely to say *ei Mann* in place of *ein Mann*, for example, just because *Mann* happens to begin with a consonant sound.

Exercise 3.6

Here are two drills on the English definite article.

Drill G

The ambassador is here.
  embassy is interesting.
  picture was new.
  music
  document

Mostly about images

Typical basic technique:

Teacher: The ambassador is here.
Students: The ambassador is here.
Teacher: Embassy.
Student 1: The embassy is here.
Teacher: Is interesting.
Student 2: The embassy is interesting.
[etc.]

Drill H

The	door of your office	is brown.
	book in my hand	is open.
	theater across the street	
	package I received yesterday	
	envelope from the travel agency	

(Basic technique as for drill G.)

1. If you were observing a class that was doing this drill, by what criteria would you judge whether or not it was going as planned?
2. What do these drills require and reward in the students' handling of mental imagery?

COMMENTS

The most conspicuous indication of whether a drill like G or H is going well is the presence or absence of a steady rhythm. If rhythm is broken either by the teacher's not being sure what is coming next, or by the teacher's going off on tangents, or by the students' having difficulty in coming up with the right responses, then something is wrong. Either the drill is simply too hard, or the teacher should explore other options (below and in Chapters 4–8) for how to conduct it.

Another thing to look for is evident interest – or boredom – on the part of students or teacher or both. To bring a very mechanical drill like G or H to life requires the teacher to *appear* to be interested in it. (This may in turn require a certain amount of acting ability on the part of the teacher!)

With regard to nonverbal imagery, these two drills look much richer than drills E and F. After all, in drill H we are talking about a book in somebody's hand, or an envelope from a travel agency. Surely these will stimulate more mental pictures than a simple list of nouns! And for some students, this may be true. Too often, however, the students' ability to image from foreign words is much less than the ability which native-

46

speaking textbook writers and teachers possess, and which teachers too readily assume in their students. When this is the case, drilling does *not* result in juxtaposition and storing of verbal–nonverbal imagery: The hoped-for new nexuses are therefore *not* formed because the nonverbal element is not there. Even for those students who do image successfully from the words of the drill, G and H are thematically so fragmented that rich, full images cannot take shape.

Exercise 3.7

1. What are some of the possible options within the basic technique sketched for drill G?

COMMENTS

With regard to technique, any blank-filling drill carries with it an option that teachers often overlook: to have the students do it orally in class before they write it as part of their homework. The advantages of doing so are that students get more practice out of that part of their textbook; they are less likely to feel confused and to make errors; and the time interval between oral and written practice is short enough so that the first makes the second easier, but long enough so that students cannot perform the second by mere parroting of the first.

Other options of technique with drills will be discussed in Chapters 4–8.

Grammar by text and task

The most serious limitation on explanations of grammar is that they are words *about* words: Whatever understanding students may have gotten from an explanation, the students do nothing to put the explanation into practice. They do not even try out their understanding of the explanation to see whether it is accurate enough to be usable.

Drills are not subject to these limitations. In a drill, students do something with words: They manipulate them. If the students' understanding of an explanation has been correct, then remembering that explanation (or that understanding!) will help to produce correct choices – correct responses to the drill. A drill can easily be designed so that it will require and reward accurate understanding of one or another selected rule or part of a rule.

We have just seen, however, that drills have serious limitations of their own. The most obvious is that the presence of suitable nonverbal imagery in the mind of a student during the usual mechanical drill is uncertain and at best fragmented. In particular, the motivational side of any drill is limited to "getting a correct answer." How can we preserve the sharpness of focus that we have seen in drills, but at the same time improve the imagery and vary the motivation? This is one of the most important practical questions in the teaching of foreign languages. It will be the subject of the rest of this chapter.

Exercise 3.8

Here is a brief exercise on the use of definite and indefinite articles (or no article at all), based on dialogs J-1 and J-2.

Exercise I

Fill in the blanks with *a, an, the,* or *some,* or leave it blank.

.... ambassador called .... few minutes ago to say that .... congresswoman is going to visit .... embassy .... next week. .... name of .... congresswoman is Alice Liddell. .... office of .... Congresswoman Liddell sent .... message saying that she would like to visit .... National Wabe.

Exercise J follows exercise I. It has the same grammatical focus but shifts to a new setting.

Exercise J

.... my sister went to work for .... large firm right after she got out of .... college. At first, she worked as .... file clerk, but a year later she became .... secretary. Soon after that, she became .... private secretary of .... senior executive, and when .... executive retired, she became .... principal staff assistant to .... president of .... company.

1. Would all native speakers agree on what should be in each of the blanks in exercises I and J?
2. How do exercises I and J compare to drills E–H with respect to imagery?
3. How do they compare to E–H with respect to the knowledge and skills that they require and reward?

48

COMMENTS

These exercises depend on the students' being able to form verbal images from words in the foreign language. In this respect they are no different from drills E–H. Because they consist of texts, however, exercises I and J have at least three advantages over a drill of about the same length: (i) In a drill, students must discard whatever nonverbal imagery they have produced for one line before going on to the next. In exercises I and J, the imagery from the first words is retained and serves as a partial basis for the nonverbal imagery that goes with the words that are to follow. (ii) Some of the conditions which determine the choice between *a* or *the* lie outside the sentence in which the choice must be made. This information is available in exercises I and J, but not in drills E–H. (iii) A text also exposes students to use of words and other devices that tie one sentence to the others: "Soon after that . . . " and the like. This cannot happen in line-by-line drills.

Exercise 3.9

Another approach to the problem of providing sharply focused verbal practice with a strong nonverbal component is the use of simple tasks to be performed in the target language. The following activity provides a few examples, again related to the use of English articles.

Activity K

Materials: a list of names of people (local or international) who are known to at least some of the students

Procedure:
a. Questions of the form "Who is [name]?" Answers of the form "................... is a congressman," "................... is the congressman from the 10th District," "a music teacher," and so on.
b. Questions of the form "Name a [former president, dry cleaner, etc.]" or "Who is the [principal of this school]?" Answers of the form "Frank Wolf," "Mr. Morrison," "Frank L. Barton," and so on. (Option: Questions may be asked first by the teacher or first by the students.)
c. Teams prepare lists of questions like those in steps (a) and (b). They then ask members of other teams these questions. The asking team gains a point if a question makes correct use of articles. The answering team gains a point for each factually correct answer, but loses a point if the answer uses articles incorrectly.

1. In what ways can this activity be called communicative (see glossary)?
2. What sorts of mental imagery does this activity require and reward?

COMMENTS

Insofar as the factual information about who is who and who is what is equally shared by all the members of the class, this activity cannot be called communicative. To some extent, however, people may have forgotten the information in (a) and (b), and in (c) each team will have introduced the need for various bits of new information. One kind of information that is being transmitted is therefore the extent to which the factual information really is shared by everyone. A second kind of information concerns the degree to which individual students control this particular range of uses of the English articles. With respect to these two types of information, the activity is communicative.

Because they are scored separately in (c) for factual and grammatical accuracy, students must use imagery concerning people and their occupations or offices. This nonverbal imagery is therefore stored in connection with the verbal imagery of the questions and answers. The motivational items that enter into the resulting nonverbal imagery include teamwork and competition, as well as the usual classroom goal of giving correct answers.

Summary

Two main points have been introduced in this chapter. One concerns the importance of thematic coherence even in relatively mechanical activities like grammar drills; this relates to nonverbal imagery. The other is the term *logogen*, which stands for the molecules of verbal imagery.

It should be clear by now that the word *imagery* is being used in a somewhat special way. Four points are worth repeating here:

1. An image does not have a physical existence or a physical basis in the same sense in which stored items have; rather, an image is a one-time result of the interaction which takes place among networks of items and among stimuli which are external to those networks. Thus when I can't remember the Portuguese word for measles but know that it has three syllables and begins with *s*, I am retrieving items without being able to generate the verbal image that I am looking for. When I appear to be retrieving the same image of a person or an incident or a word day after day, it is because very much the same networks are interacting with very much the same external stimuli.
2. An image is not merely visual. It may include any dimension – sight, hearing, texture, weight, temperature, motion, time, purpose, emo-

tion, and many others – and commonly includes more than one of these dimensions at the same time.

3. The essential thing about an image is not that it is more or less vividly perceived (Dickel and Slak 1983), but that it is a basis for action – for drawing a map of the place where I was yesterday, or for constructing a subjunctive verb form, or for knowing when a subjunctive form is required, or for supplying the right word for what I want to name. Such an image may be more or less complete, more or less accurate, more or less "solid," more or less rapidly available.

4. Images are not to be valued in language study for their own sake. They are valuable because the process of generating them involves activating old nexuses and establishing new ones among networks of items which will be needed for generating images – both nonverbal and verbal – on future occasions; and because the rewards that come from having generated them strengthen the nexuses and make the networks more solid, more complete, and more usable.

In the literature

On the giving of explanations about grammar (exercise 3.2), see Rivers and Temperley (1978).

In connection with exercise 3.3, Stevick (1980: 253, 255) contains further discussion of the relationship between those who ask questions and those who give answers about the grammar of foreign languages. The style of response recommended in (i) and (ii) in the comments section allows the teacher to become what Ahsen (1981: 165) calls an "immediator" rather than just an instructor.

On the relationship between understanding and using grammar, see Rivers (1983: 35–6).

Warren (1972, 1974) derived the idea of logogens (exercise 3.4) from an earlier article by Morton (1969). As Warren used the term, memory contains (among other things) a number of these units, at each of which is stored the motor program for the production of the word that it represents. In a later treatment of the concept, Morton and Patterson (1980) postulate separate input and output logogens, and separate auditory- versus visual-input logogens.

In regard to exercise 3.5, it has been well established that certain words are much more powerful than others in calling up nonverbal imagery (see Paivio, Yuille, and Madigan 1968). For a discussion of the relationship among (verbal) images, patterns, and rules, see Stevick (1982: 31ff).

Among the many treatments of drill types such as E–H are Paulston and Bruder (1975), Rivers and Temperley (1978: 125ff), and

Stevick (1982: ch. 8–10). Another treatment of drills is Cook (1982). Diller (1978) discusses contrasting approaches to language teaching in general, and is excellent.

There has been a great deal of experimental research on the importance of the length of time between two occurrences of a given word or other item to be practiced (see comments on exercise 3.7). This research has generally indicated that people retain more as a result of a given number of exposures to new verbal material if the time that passes between successive exposures is neither too short nor too long. See for example Ciccone (1973) and Meredith (1978). I referred to this principle on page 48 of *Teaching and Learning Languages* (1982).

The importance of thematic integrity in language practice (exercise 3.5) is emphasized in Oller and Richard-Amato (1983), especially in Chapter 1. For discussion of the devices of coherence and cohesion, see Oller (1983). The importance of "rich and continuing project-like activity" is a major theme of Brumfit (1984, especially pp. 118–22).

The blank-filling activity in exercise 3.8 is a rudimentary example of the cloze procedure, which has found increasing use in language teaching during the past 30 years, for testing as well as for teaching. Basic information about cloze may be found in Greenwald (1981), van Parreren and Schouten-van Parreren (1981), Heilenman (1983), Soudek and Soudek (1983), Brown (1983), and Celce-Murcia (1985).

The need to switch occasionally to a focus on linguistic form is treated by Raimes (1983: 55–6) and Widdowson (1983: 30). For discussion of simple activities with sharp grammatical focus (exercise 3.9), see Galyean (1977). A two-volume set which contains many specific ideas is Wilson and Wattenmaker (1980a, b).

Part II Mostly about options

Chapters 1–3 consisted of exercises which were based either on activiti unrelated to the teaching and learning of languages or on artificial less materials which had been written to illustrate a series of points. T purpose of those chapters was to develop a set of concepts about roles of verbal and nonverbal imagery.

The rest of this book will focus on options which are open to teach who are aware of how imagery works in the minds of their studer Each chapter explores the possibilities of some set or sets of publish materials. These materials have been chosen to represent a variety levels, formats, and publishers. As in Part I, readers will derive maxim benefit from the exercises if they go through them in the compan two or three other teachers.

After you have worked your way through the exercises, you sh be familiar with these options and be able to make appropriate ch among them to suit your own class. Nobody else can do this for teacher. Using a succession of combinations of alternatives from a range of options will not only allow you to respond better to your It will also allow your students to get more practice on each point wi feeling that they are stuck too long on one thing. Finally, it will in your students' confidence in you, and this will further enhance learning!

4 A pre-beginners' textbook

Before Book One, by John Boyd and Mary Ann Boyd, was published by Regents in 1982. At that time I was teaching a group of Central American refugees, some of whom knew no English and a few of whom were barely literate in Spanish. I was also serving as adviser to a number of untrained teachers who were working with the same group or with one closely related to it. We found *Before Book One* to be highly suited to our needs. The options which I will describe in this chapter therefore grew out of actual classroom experiences.

The authors of *Before Book One* point out that many so-called beginning texts are really for false beginners and that such texts actually presuppose a little knowledge of English. An absolute beginner who finds himself or herself in a class that uses such a text may be easily overwhelmed and so become discouraged. The Boyds' solution is to take advantage of the fact that people can come to understand language much more easily and quickly than they can learn to produce it correctly, and that the experience of producing appropriate responses *to* a new language without having to produce them *through the words* of that language can enhance a student's morale.

Before Book One is based on three assumptions:

1. Some students know no English at all.
2. A good way for these and most other students to begin is through comprehension exercises. There are four essential elements in a comprehension exercise:
   a. Students listen to a series of utterances in the new language.
   b. Students respond to each bit in some way.
   c. Each response is accurate or inaccurate with reference to some set of *external facts*.
   d. These responses may consist of pointing, or other physical actions, or words in the students' native language, or a *very* few *very* simple words in the target language. Except for these very simple words, the students' replies do not require them to use the target language.
3. Students need to have clearly in mind the meaning of what they are hearing or saying while they are hearing it or saying it.

Mostly about options

Before Book One is an appropriate first-level text for students from any first-language background who enter an ESL class without prior study of or exposure to English. No one is at too low a level to use the material. Because it sharpens aural skills while easing students into the language-learning environment, it can serve as an introductory text to any ESL or literacy series. This was the audience for whom the book was originally intended. Used in another way, however, the book can provide rapid-paced and satisfying work for students who are literate in the roman alphabet and who have already picked up a small amount of English. Most of our students actually fell into this second category.

Exercise 4.1

Figure 4.1 is a reproduction of page 1 from Lesson 1.

1. How might you use this page with beginners who know only the spoken words and the written figures for 0–9? (The authors of *Before Book One* actually suggest ways of teaching even the numerals, but we will omit those techniques here.)
2. How might you use this page with false beginners who know numbers of up to 1,000?
3. How do your answers to (1) and (2) differ?
4. Compare your ideas with the ideas of the other people in your group.

COMMENTS

Your answers to (3) and (4) will bring out a number of choices, or *options*, which are available to any language teacher. My intent in this chapter and the remaining chapters will not be to prescribe one alternative or to reject another. It will be rather to help readers to find the alternatives and to explore the potential advantages of each. I believe that the choice between alternatives should be made not by the writer of a book like this one, but by the practicing teacher.

The suggestions in this chapter take into account two contrasting but mutually complementary principles: the need for predictability in what we do, and the value of unpredictability. If students have to spend too much of their time and mental energy figuring out what kind of activity is coming next, they can quickly become confused, tired, and discouraged. Working without a familiar and dependable routine can cause extra fatigue for the teacher, too, of course.

On the other hand, as we all know, too much predictability leads to monotony and loss of attention, and students can lose the feeling that they are making progress. There is thus a place in lesson planning both

PART 1

1. 334	332	331
2. 221	222	225
3. 553	554	551
4. 112	114	113
5. 454	434	424
6. 312	213	321
7. 453	345	534
8. 152	215	521

PART 2

1. _____

2. _____

3. _____

4. _____

5. _____

6. _____

7. _____

8. _____

9. _____

10. _____

Figure 4.1. Page 1 from Lesson 1 in *Before Book One*, Student's Book, by John Boyd and Mary Ann Boyd. (Reproduced with permission. ©1982 by Regents Publishing Company.)

for a few recurring themes and for some interesting variations. The goal is to combine reassurance with stimulation, and certainty with interest.

Exercise 4.2

In the procedure suggested in the Teacher's Manual for *Before Book One*, the teacher calls out one number sequence from each row in Part 1. Students listen and circle the number that they think they heard. The numbers are to be read "three-three-four," etc.

One exceedingly important option with *Before Book One* is whether or not to have the students write in the book, as in Part 2 on page 1.

1. What are the advantages of each choice?
2. What are the imagery implications?

OPTION 1: WHETHER STUDENTS SHOULD WRITE IN THEIR BOOKS

a. You may decide to have students write in their books as you go through an activity. Two advantages are: (i) Many students are accustomed to doing this kind of thing. (ii) They will take home a permanent record of what they have done. When students write, they are required to repeat to themselves at least silently the spoken words that are involved, produce the corresponding physical acts with hand and pencil, and see the results of what hand and pencil have done. All three of these sets of data are available for storage with one another. If we can believe their reports about themselves, students differ drastically in their ability to profit both from the physical act of writing and from the opportunity to go back and look at what they have written. Some claim to find writing almost an absolute necessity, others can take it or leave it, and a few find it only a nuisance.

b. On the other hand, you may have students refrain from writing in the books. Advantages: (i) The books can be used with other classes, at a considerable saving of money. (ii) Even within a single class session, you have greater flexibility for using and reusing the materials, and thereby get more mileage per page. (iii) You avoid the nuisance of having to check written work at a time when the main goal is development of comprehension.

Exercise 4.3

If students are not to make written responses, then they must of course respond orally.

1. How can they do this without having to repeat after the teacher and thus violate the underlying principle of this set of lessons?

COMMENTS

One system that worked very well for my colleagues and me was to assign the letters *A, B,* and *C* to the three columns of numbers on the printed page. Then students could reply "3-B" to show that they had heard "554," for example. It is true that these responses are in the target language, but they require only the smallest and simplest repertoire, and students' pronunciation of them is not commented on.

Exercise 4.4

One brand of pedagogical orthodoxy demands that students respond immediately, and if possible without thinking, to each task as it comes from the lips of the teacher.

1. What are the alternatives, and the advantages of each?
2. Discuss this question with the other members of your group.

OPTION 2: WHETHER OR NOT TO ALLOW AN IMMEDIATE RESPONSE

a. Have students respond immediately to your questions, readings of numbers, and so on. Advantages: (i) This is what people do instinctively – or at least it's what they try to do! It may therefore be more comfortable. (ii) It saves a little time.
b. Have students wait a few seconds, until you give them a signal, before you call on them to reply. Advantages: (i) People have a few seconds in which to let their ears process what they have heard. (ii) The slower students are not at such a disadvantage. (iii) If you are calling on individuals, this keeps everyone maximally alert.

Exercise 4.5

Again imagine yourself teaching page 1 of *Before Book One.*

1. Are your students responding in unison, or individually? Compare your imagined class with the imagined classes of the other members of your group.
2. What choices do you have regarding student response?

OPTION 3: CHORAL RESPONSE VERSUS INDIVIDUAL RESPONSE

a. Have the whole class respond in unison. Advantage: Individuals can answer aloud, using their voices and storing in memory the kinesthetic and auditory results of having done so, and they can do this with less risk of personal exposure.
b. Have them answer individually. Advantages: (i) You can find out who is saying what. (ii) Individuals can find out whether their answers were right.

Exercise 4.6

When students answer individually, you must find some way of letting them know whose turn it is.

1. What are your alternatives in deciding who responds next?
2. What are the advantages of each alternative?
3. Compare your replies with the replies of the other members of your group.

OPTION 4: ORDER OF STUDENT RESPONSE

a. The simplest way to let students know when it's their turn is to go around the class in some predictable order: clockwise or counter-clockwise or front row left-to-right, then second row right-to-left, and so on. These are only three of the numerous subalternatives within this alternative. Many teachers always call on their students in a fixed order, and some defend it as the only way. It certainly has the advantages of minimizing student insecurity, of allowing the activity to move along smoothly, and of ensuring an equitable distribution of chances to participate. I use it sometimes.
b. The other choice is to call on students in some irregular order that they cannot predict. Teachers who prefer this alternative argue that it keeps students on their toes. Anyone who has ever observed a student counting the students ahead and then locating the one sentence that he or she is going to get and ignoring the rest can appreciate this advantage. A second advantage is that by steering the harder tasks to other people, you can protect students who appear anxious.

Exercise 4.7

Calling on students in random order presents a further set of alternatives.

1. What practices for calling on students randomly have you seen or used?
2. Compare your experiences with those of other members of your group.

OPTION 5: CALLING ON STUDENTS

a. One alternative is to designate students by name. To do so is more personal and more courteous. Under some circumstances this can be an advantage. It certainly seems to be the alternative that many inexperienced teachers select instinctively.
b. Another alternative is to point or nod to students. This must of course be done within the restrictions which the students' native cultures place on such gestures, or it may give offense. In situations where it can be used, it does have four potential advantages: (i) It is silent, and so does not insert irrelevant audible material into the sequence of activity. (ii) It saves time. (iii) It requires students to watch the teacher, instead of letting them bury themselves in their books. (iv) Using a person's name is a way of exerting control over that person. Avoiding names sometimes leaves students with less feeling of personal exposure. Superimposed on alternatives (a) and (b) is a choice between:
c. Mentioning the name or making the gesture before you identify the task: "Eduardo, 331." The advantage is that the person who is to respond has a chance to focus his attention fully on the task, which here is to understand "331" and reply by identifying the correct number.
d. Identify the task before indicating who is to respond. As often happens, the advantage of one alternative is the mirror image of the advantage of the other: Everyone has to focus on the task and do it mentally, instead of being able to tune out as soon as someone else's name is called. This is particularly effective if you allow two or three seconds to elapse between the task and the name, as in option 2b.

Exercise 4.8

Some teachers use what I call the "double index" method with their students: They move their left index finger down the page, and their right index finger from one student to the next. In so doing, they miss some useful options. (For this exercise, assume that you do *not* have the students write in the workbook.)

1. With regard to page 1 of *Before Book One*, what choices do you have in how you move from one item to the next?
2. What are the advantages of each way?

OPTION 6: MOVING THROUGH THE MATERIALS

a. Work down the page one row at a time, using the items in each horizontal row in random order, but using each of them at least once before going on to the next row. Advantage: Students know pretty much where you are at all times, and can therefore concentrate on listening to new and unfamiliar items.
b. Use only one item from each horizontal row, still going down the page one row at a time. Advantage: Students get a feeling of acceleration without danger of getting lost.
c. Use items at random from anywhere within a single section of the unit. Advantage: Students often find this an invigorating challenge.

SUMMARY COMMENTS

We have used the first page of an extremely low-level set of materials in order to develop some very elementary but important options. Any one of these options is useful to know about, but their real power lies in the fact that you can combine them in so many ways. Counting only three of the many possible subalternatives in option 4 (order of student response), options 4 and 5 (order of student response, calling on students) provide seven different ways of calling on students. Multiply these by the three ways of moving through page 1 (option 6), and we have 21 workable combinations.

Exercise 4.9

A transcript of a few minutes from a hypothetical class session follows the questions to this exercise.

1. As you read the transcript, imagine yourself in the role of the teacher.
2. What options are you using from moment to moment? Mark the options where they change.
3. At what points, if any, would you prefer to use options different from the ones shown here?
4. Compare your answers to (1)–(3) with the answers of the other members of your group.

Here is a seating diagram of the class:

13	14	15	16
9	10	11	12
5	6	7	8
1	2	3	4

T

Here is a key to the abbreviations in the transcript:
T (teacher)   C (class in unison)   S7 (student 7)
(serial number of line)   ...(more of the same)

T#01: 334.
C#02: 1-A.
T#03: 331.
C#04: 1-C.
T#05: 332.
C#06: 1-B.
T#07: 221.
C#08: 2-A.
T#09: 222.
C#10: 2-B.
T#11: 225.
C#12: 2-C.
...
T#13: 521.
C#14: 8-C.
T#15: 152.
C#16: 8-A.
T#17: 332.
C#18: 1-B.
T#19: 225.
C#20: 2-C.
T#21: 551.
C#22: 3-C.
...
T#23: 152.
C#24: 8-A.
T#25: 114.
C#26: 4-B.
T#27: 534.
C#28: 7-C.
...
T#29: 113.
C#30: 4-C.
T#31: S1, 334.
S1#32: 1-A.
T#33: S2, 332.

S2#34: 1-B.
T#35: S3, 334.
S3#36: 1-A.
T#37: S4, #331.
S4#38: 1-C.
T#39: S-8, 225.
S8#40: 2-C.
T#41: S-7, 225.
S7#42: 2-C.
T#43: S-6, 221.
S6#44: 2-A.
T#45: S-5, 222.
S5#46: 2-B.
T#47: S-9, 321.
S9#48: 6-C.
T#49: S10, 454.
S10#50: 5-A.
T#51: S11, 551.
S11#52: 3-C.
T#53: 215.
S12#54: 8-B.
T#55: 453.
S16#56: 7-A.
T#57: 424.
S15#58: 5-C.
T#59: 312.
S14#60: 6-A.
T#61: 213.
S2#62: 6-B.
T#63: 551.
S7#64: 3-C.
T#65: 332.
S10#66: 1-B.

COMMENTS

As we saw in exercise 2.3, four conditions seem to help a new item or distinction to establish itself in the awareness of a learner: (1) The learner has some occasion to notice the new item or distinction. (2) The learner's brain has time to process the new information. (3) The learner is required to respond in some way to the new item or distinction. (4) The learner receives some kind of reward or other informative feedback to the response made in (3).

Doing exercise 4.9 requires care and patience, because you have to look at each line of abstract symbols and construct your own nonverbal imagery of what is going on in the class. (Did you find the changes at lines 13, 17, 25, 31, 53, and 61?) This exercise is in fact an attempt to provide the preceding four conditions not only for the specific options we have examined so far, but also for the more general principle that countless options about as useful as these exist at all times in the language classroom. Later in this book we will consider other ways in which we may provide the same four conditions for our students.

Exercise 4.10

Up to this point, we have ignored a choice that any teacher would have available in actually using page 1 of *Before Book One* with a class. How is the teacher to pronounce "334"?

1. What are the alternatives? What are the advantages of each alternative?
2. Which would you use first?
3. Discuss (1) and (2) with the other members of your group.

OPTION 7: WHAT REGISTER OF LANGUAGE TO USE

a. Be maximally clear; for example, read them one digit at a time: "three-three-four," and so on. Advantages: (i) This is the simplest because it does not require students to understand words like *hundred* or *thirty*. (ii) It is what students will meet when people give phone numbers.

b. Read them naturally but carefully; for example, using the names of multiples of ten: "three hundred and thirty-four," and so on. Advantage: The names of the multiples of ten are extremely common in everyday life. This form is used in talking about populations, distances, weights, and so forth, as well as in giving numbers as numbers.

c. Read them in a natural and relaxed way. For example, you could read them in abbreviated fashion: "three thirty-four," and so on. Advantages: (i) This form is the most difficult, and hence handling the numbers successfully can give people a feeling of accomplishment. (ii) It is the form that students will meet when people talk about prices ($3.34 or $334.99), addresses, and hotel rooms.

COMMENTS

Option 7 is quite specialized with reference to this particular page of this particular lesson. Its general principle, however, is that people say "the same thing" in different ways depending on circumstances. For this reason, we will call it the "register option" and use it in a more general way later on.

Exercise 4.11

Up to this point, the teacher has been initiating every exchange with the students.

1. How is the teacher's monopoly of initiative likely to affect the images that the students will form in their own minds?
2. What alternatives does the teacher have to this monopoly if the class consists of absolute beginners?

OPTION 8: WHO TAKES THE INITIATIVE

a. You take the initiative in speaking first or in selecting which item the students are to try next. Advantage: Things move at a smoother rate, which is under your control.
b. The students speak first or select which item to try next. This can be done even with beginners after a little teacher-initiated practice. Advantages: (i) Students hear what they are most aware of needing at the moment. (ii) It takes the students out of the situation where they are always reacting to your initiatives, and gives them a small but real bit of power. You, of course, still retain the power of calling on students to exercise initiative, so that this option need not degenerate into sitting and waiting for someone to do something.

When students take the initiative in this activity, the meaning of what is to be said is in their minds *before* the words are produced. After they have produced the words, they observe your behavior in order to see whether the intended meaning was satisfactorily conveyed. This is quite a different process from hearing noises from you and then scrambling, first to find the meaning that fits those noises, and then to say "4-C" or whatever corresponds to that meaning. Here is one of the imagery implications of this option.

Another is the difference between storing in memory, along with the noises and the meanings, either the feeling that "my role in this language is to react to what someone else says to me" or the feeling

65

that "my role in this language is to get other people to react to me in ways that I intend." It goes without saying that a well-balanced course should ensure that students store items of both these kinds.

Exercise 4.12

You don't have to limit yourself to what is on page 1 of *Before Book One*. You can put the numerals into phrases or sentences.

1. Give some examples of how this might be done.
2. What are the advantages of limiting yourself to what is in the book or putting the numerals into phrases?
3. Discuss (1) and (2) with the other members of your group.

OPTION 9: WHETHER TO HIDE THE WORDS THAT THE ACTIVITY IS ABOUT

a. Read aloud nothing but the numbers. Advantages: (i) The class moves more quickly, with more student turns per minute. (ii) The word targets that students are to identify stand out clearly.
b. Embed the numbers in a short expression: "Number 334," "Where is 551?" "424 people," "page 225," and so on. Advantages: (i) This is closer to what students will meet outside the classroom. (ii) It provides a feeling of extra challenge and therefore of extra achievement. This feeling can contribute to a feeling of excitement, and of course this feeling also gets stored along with the words and their meanings – emotional items which will participate in the overall memory composite.
c. Embed the numbers in longer expressions: "I think it's 334 miles from here to Denver," and so on. The advantages are as for (b), but the distinction between long and short expressions is one that students respond to, and so it is worth listing separately here.

OPTION 10, A SUPER OPTION: WHETHER TO AIM FOR SECURITY OR FOR CHALLENGE

a. Begin with the least demanding option and move toward more challenging ones. Advantage: You are less likely to leave students confused or discouraged.
b. Begin with an option that you think will challenge students without discouraging them or hopelessly confusing them. If it turns out that you have been overoptimistic, you can always move back to simpler options. Advantages: (i) You are less likely to spend time on work which is too easy for your students, and which therefore seems to

A pre-beginners' textbook

them to be a waste of time. (ii) If you succeed with this alternative in option 10, students come out with increased self-respect and self-confidence.

A summary of all the options in this book is found in the appendix at the back of the book. Remember that the real flexibility and power in the use of these options comes when you use more than one alternative of each option in various combinations in successive steps of your technique.

Summary exercise 4.13

In exercise 4.9, we were working with a total of 21 alternatives. Options 7–9 (register, initiative, and hiding words) have added respectively 3, 2, and 3 more alternatives. The new total number of combinations is now $3 \times 2 \times 3 \times 21$, or 378. The super option further multiplies these possibilities.

1. Which combination of the alternatives in options 1–9 (see list in the appendix) is represented in each of the sequences given below?

   Sequence A:
   Student 9: Three-four-five.
   Teacher: 7-B.
   Student 10: Five-five-three.
   Teacher: 3-A.
   Answers: 1b, 2a, 3b, 4a, 5bc, 6c, 7a, 8b, 9a

   Sequence B:
   Teacher: Three hundred and forty-five dollars. (*pause*)
   Student 5: 7-B.
   Teacher: Page five hundred and fifty-three. (*pause*)
   Student 11: 3-A.
   Answers: ....

   Sequence C:
   Student 15: Room three forty-five.
   Teacher: 7-B.
   Student 15: Room five thirty-four.
   Teacher: 7-C.
   Answers: ....

2. Referring to page 1 of *Before Book One*, write a 4-line sequence to illustrate each of the following combinations (a dash means to ignore this option).
   A. 1b, 2b, 3a, 4a, 5ad, 6a, 7b, 8a, 9a

Mostly about options

B.　1a,　2a,　3b,　4b,　5bd,　6b,　7c,　8a,　9c
C.　–,　2b,　–,　–,　–,　6c,　7a,　8b,　9b

3. Using the super option (option 10, whether to aim for security or for challenge) make a single change in each of these three sequences that will make it a little bit easier. Then make changes that will make each sequence a little bit more challenging.
4. Discuss your answers with the other members of your group.
5. Write a series of two or three sequences which you think would go well together. Exchange with other members of your group and identify the alternatives that have been used.

COMMENTS

As in exercise 4.9, the object here is to help you build your own stock of imagery about technique by giving you the occasion, time, and feedback for noticing small distinctions. What is important here is not the options themselves, or the combinations of options. It is rather the habit of looking at techniques in terms of their components. Again, this takes patience, but again it can be time and effort well spent! Obviously you won't use all of these combinations in a given class session. On the other hand, there are two good reasons for using as many as a dozen of them in a single session: (a) As your students work through the exercise, they will become able to do things that they could not have done when they began. For this reason, the combination of alternatives that was appropriate at the beginning will rapidly become less appropriate. (b) The very fact that they see you changing techniques will come to the students as an expression of *your confidence in them*. (They may also be impressed by your technical proficiency, and this will be good for them because it will build *their confidence in you*.)

At the same time, however, remember that options are best used in reference to some familiar basic technique with which both you and your students are comfortable.

You can apply the same principles over and over again as you work your way through this book, first identifying and then combining the choices that are available to you. Details will of course be slightly different for each activity. In the remainder of this chapter we will work briefly with two more pages from *Before Book One*, adding a few new options and also reapplying the first ten.

Exercise 4.14

Figure 4.2 is a reproduction of page 4 in *Before Book One*. The Teacher's Manual that comes with the book instructs the teacher to read each telephone number aloud once at a normal rate of speed and to have the

68

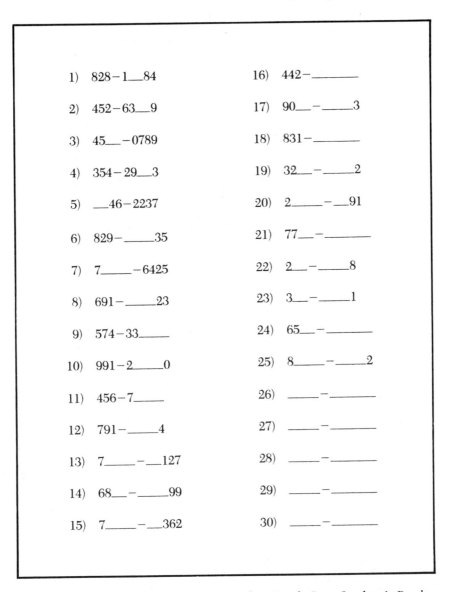

1) 828 – 1__84

2) 452 – 63__9

3) 45__ – 0789

4) 354 – 29__3

5) __46 – 2237

6) 829 – ____35

7) 7____ – 6425

8) 691 – ____23

9) 574 – 33____

10) 991 – 2____0

11) 456 – 7____

12) 791 – ____4

13) 7____ – __127

14) 68__ – ____99

15) 7____ – __362

16) 442 – _____

17) 90__ – ____3

18) 831 – _____

19) 32__ – ____2

20) 2____ – __91

21) 77__ – _____

22) 2__ – ____8

23) 3__ – ____1

24) 65__ – _____

25) 8____ – ____2

26) ____ – _____

27) ____ – _____

28) ____ – _____

29) ____ – _____

30) ____ – _____

Figure 4.2. Page 4 from Lesson 1 in *Before Book One*, Student's Book, by John Boyd and Mary Ann Boyd. (Reproduced with permission. ©1982 by Regents Publishing Company.)

students fill in the missing figures. Then the teacher is to write the full telephone numbers on the board and say them aloud so that students can check their work. That is certainly a sensible and effective way to use this page.

1. What alternatives does this technique use from options 1–9 (see list of options in the appendix)?
2. About how many minutes do you think it would take to go through page 4 in this way?
3. Check your answers to (1) and (2) with other members of your group.
4. Suggest other techniques which would get two or three times as many minutes from the same page. Then compare your ideas with the ideas of the other members of your group.
5. Did your replies to (4) include option 8b (student initiative)? If not, how could you use this alternative with page 4 of *Before Book One*?

Exercise 4.15

Here is a sequence that might be used with page 4 of *Before Book One*. Read through it, imagining yourself as the teacher. See exercise 4.9 for a key to the abbreviations used.

(Books are open to p. 4.)
T#01: 828–1 uhhh 84. S01, give me a number, please.
S01#02: 9.
T#03: Thank you! 828–1984. *(motioning to class)* Write this in your books, please. *(to S01) This is your number! (to class)* S01's number is 828–1984! *(Teacher enters the number and name in his or her own book.)*
T#04: S02, give me a number!
S02#05: 7.
T#06: 7! All right! 452–6379! S02's number is 452–6379! *(Teacher checks to see that all have filled in the blank accordingly.)*
[And so on, for all members of the class.]
T#07: Who has number 452–6379?
C#08: S02!
T#09: S02! And who has 354–2903!
C#10: S04!
T#11: *(Looking at S01 and pretending to use a telephone. Tone of voice may be urgent or excited.)* Hello! Hello! Is this 828–1984?
S01#12: Yes.
T#13: I'd like to speak with S01! Is this S01?
S01#14: Yes.

T#15: Oh, good! How are you, S01?
S01#16: Very well.
T#17: Good. Well, good-bye, S01!
S01#18: Good-bye. *(They hang up.)*
  [Repeat with other students.]
T#19: *(looking at S02 and again pretending to use phone)* Hello! Hello!
  Is this 354–2903 [or 452–6319]?
S02#20: No.
T#21: Oh! I'm sorry! *(Hangs up and tries again.)* [And so on until each
  person has been spoken with at least once.]

This sequence illustrates option 8b (student initiative), as well as a few
new options.

OPTION 11: WHETHER TO PERSONALIZE

a. Use the material from the book without attaching it to individual
   students. Advantages: (i) Doing so requires less time and imagination.
   (ii) Attaching language to students too often can seem artificial and
   even annoying.
b. Attach various parts of the material to different students, as in the
   preceding sequence. Advantages: (i) Doing so seems to lead to a
   pleasant kind of arousal on the part of the students. This may serve
   to hold attention. (ii) It may lead to improved learning. (Some studies
   of memory have shown that people hold on to things better if they
   think there is some connection either with themselves or with some
   important individual, possibly because it ties the material in with
   fuller, more active networks, as this term is used in Chapter 1.)
     If all of the students have telephones, it would of course be possible
   to use their numbers in an activity that either replaced or supplemented the one on page 4 of *Before Book One*. Advantages: As in
   (a). Disadvantages: Some people are reluctant to give their phone
   numbers to relative strangers, so that asking them to do so might
   provoke anxiety.

OPTION 12: WHETHER TO DRAMATIZE

a. "Play it straight," as in lines 1–10 of the sequence. Advantage: This
   is the more businesslike way to do it, and therefore may leave some
   students feeling more secure.
b. Treat the material with a little pizzazz. As illustrated in lines 11–21,
   for example, put the material into a brief role play which makes
   minimum demands on the student's ability to produce the target
   language. Advantages: (i) This activates networks of items which the
   student already has in storage relative to the use of a telephone, and

71

so on. (ii) It is more challenging linguistically, emotionally, and personally. Successful participation in such an exchange can therefore leave a student with enhanced self-confidence.

OPTION 13: WHETHER TO MAKE ERRORS OF FACT

In line 19 of the sequence, the teacher made an error of fact. Most of the students probably recognized that the error was intentional.

a. Avoid making errors. Advantage: To make too many errors would be disruptive.
b. Make occasional errors of *fact*. Advantages: (i) Even though students suspect that the errors are intentional, they may still take some comfort in the fact that they are not the only ones who are sometimes wrong. They get a chance to correct the teacher! (ii) The prospect of such errors requires the students to pay closer attention to what you say. (iii) An occasional error contributes to a sense of fun in the class. (Factual errors are to be differentiated from errors of *language* – mispronouncing words, or producing incorrect grammar. To do so would at best be a waste of time. At worst, the students might learn and use the wrong forms.)

1. All teachers (except very strict and very expert practitioners of the Silent Way, a method developed by Caleb Gattegno) use their voices, but few seem to be aware of the contrasting manners which they have available for using them. What are some of these manners?
2. What would be the advantages of each in teaching page 4 of *Before Book One?*

OPTION 14: HOW TO USE YOUR VOICE

a. Speak slowly in a very firm voice, making frequent eye contact with your students. Advantage: Students can hear more clearly, which can enhance their confidence.
b. Speak at normal speed and in a relaxed voice. Advantage: Students get a chance to hear language which is closer to what they are likely to run into outside the classroom. If they succeed in following it, the experience can enhance their confidence even more than (a) can.
c. Speak rapidly and indistinctly, perhaps talking into a drinking glass or an empty coffee can in order to distort your voice. Advantages: (i) This can be done playfully, with all the emotional and social benefits that play can contribute to the class. (ii) Again, if students succeed in following you under these circumstances, the experience will build their confidence for the telephone and other out-of-class situations even more than (b) can. (I have seen quite a variety of students respond well to this alternative.)

Summary exercise 4.16

With the other members of your group, discuss the pros and cons of the alternatives in options 11–14 (personalizing, dramatizing, making factual errors, use of teacher's voice).

Exercise 4.17

Another important option is how much to ask students to contribute at the very beginning of the lesson. Figure 4.3 is a reproduction of page 29 in *Before Book One* from Lesson 3, "Clothes and Things."

1. What kinds of things might you guess a class of near-beginners would know if they were literate in languages that use the roman alphabet?
2. How might you allow them to use this knowledge?
3. What would be some of the advantages of being cautious in this regard? What would be the advantages of being adventurous?

OPTION 15: WHAT TO ASSUME ABOUT THE STUDENTS' ABILITY

a. Assume that students have no ability either to produce or to comprehend what is in the lesson. For example, begin by pointing to each item on page 29 of *Before Book One* in turn, having the students repeat it after you, and then write the word(s) on the board for them. This is the alternative suggested in the Teacher's Manual. Advantage: It is close to what people are accustomed to from earlier school experiences, so students will be able to follow the procedure more easily.

b. Assume that although the students cannot produce much of the new material independently yet, they can at least recognize some of it and then produce what they have recognized. For example, begin by giving the students a written list of the names of items pictured (perhaps with a few extra words that are not illustrated on the page), and have the students identify which is which. Advantage: People don't have to grope for new words, but they still have the challenge of matching the words with pictures.

c. Assume that students may already be able to come up with some of the material that is to be covered in the lesson, and give them an opportunity to do so. For example, begin by asking students how many of the objects on the page they can name. Advantages: (i) This gives you information about the level of your students relative to this particular unit. (ii) It gives students both an opportunity to use what

Figure 4.3. Page 29 from Lesson 3 in *Before Book One,* Student's Book, by John Boyd and Mary Ann Boyd. (Reproduced with permission. ©1982 by Regents Publishing Company.)

they already know, and a feeling of being recognized for having known it. (iii) It leaves students with more of a sense of involvement with what is on the page.

Exercise 4.18

There follows a sequence based on a session that I taught using page 29 of *Before Book One*. The students were not absolute beginners, but their English was still well below what could be called the intermediate level. I wanted them to use the nine words in meaningful and communicative (see Chapter 1) ways, but I did not want to require them to use many words except those that they were hearing from me. (See exercise 4.9 for a key to the abbreviations used.)

1. Which options are illustrated, and where do the alternatives change?
2. Amplify and improve the sequence by using other alternatives from options 1–15 (see list in appendix).
3. Amplify and improve the sequence by using your own ideas.
4. Discuss (1)–(3) with the other members of your group.

T#01: *(to class, pointing to page)* What do you see?
S04#02: Table.
T#03: A table! Right! *(writing on board)* A table! That's number...?
S04#04: 3.
T#05: A table! Number 3. *(pointing)* Right! And what else?
S02#06: Number 2. Vet.
T#07: A bed! Yes! Number 2. *(writing)* A bed!
S05#08: Llave.
T#09: Yes! A key! *(writing)* A key! *(to class)* Number?
Ss02 & 05#10: 6.
T#11: *(pointing)* Number 6 is a key!
...
T#12: S05, how many keys do you have?
S05#13: *(counting)* Four.
T#14: *(to class)* S05 has four keys. S01, how many keys do you have?
S01#15: I...has...three...
T#16: You have three keys? *(S01 #17 nods.)*
T#18: *(to class)* S01 has three keys!
...
T#19: *(to class)* Which is heavier *(pantomiming)*, a key or a chair?
C#20: A chair.
T#21: A chair! A chair is heavier than a key.
...

T#22: And which is heavier, a key or a comb? [There was difference of opinion, with about half of the class voting in either direction. Finally we asked for a key and a comb from members of the class, and had several people compare their weights by taking them in their hands. This still did not produce unanimity.]
...

T#23: What color is your favorite chair? *(Nods to S03.)*
S03#24: Brown.
S05#25: *(to T)* What color you favorite chair?
T#26: My favorite chair? What color is my favorite chair?
S05#27: *(nods)*
T#28: My favorite chair is *(dramatic pause)* green!
...

COMMENTS

With regard to imagery, my central purpose in this sequence was to have students store, along with the nine words, a wide variety of nonverbal items having to do with ownership, weight, color, and so on. Other items included purposes – talking about oneself, making judgments – which are not found in conventional classroom recitation. There was also a certain amount of fun associated with the great key–comb controversy.

On another level also related to imagery, I was exposing the students to verbal material (words and sentence patterns) which was beyond the lesson as planned by the authors of *Before Book One*. The students already controlled enough of the verbal items contained in these words and phrases so that they could comprehend my meanings, but they did not yet have enough items to enable them to produce the same words and sentence patterns correctly. I was thus laying the groundwork for future speaking by the students, but without requiring them to use the new words and phrases at this time. (See Krashen and Terrell 1983 on "comprehensible input at i + 1.")

Summary

The format of *Before Book One* is slightly unusual, but to my firsthand knowledge it is highly effective, and it has served as an excellent medium in which to develop a number of basic options which are available to language teachers in working with many other formats, and with intermediate and advanced students as well as with beginners. These same options will show up again in the chapters that follow. You will get the full power out of these options when within a single technique you use *more than one alternative* per option, in a series of combinations and recombinations.

In the literature

There is a growing literature on the advantages of having students hear and respond to large amounts of comprehensible input before they begin to speak. Two articles by Dirven and Oakeshott-Taylor (1985) survey the state of the art in listening comprehension. See, among others, the entire issue of *Foreign Language Annals* 17(4), the entire issue of *System* 11(3), Met (1984), Krashen and Terrell (1983), and Grellet (1981). Bracken (1981) presents evidence that people both get clearer images for personalized sentences (option 11) and also recall such sentences better. Omaggio (1982) is also of great interest on this point.

Gerngross and Puchta's discussion (1984: 93) of the importance of the teacher's personality makes clear one reason why option 12b (dramatizing) is so important. Raimes's technique of brainstorming (1983: 69) is a good illustration of option 15c, in which the students' previously existing resources both contribute to the work of the class and are made more available because of that work. Some instructive examples of option 12b (dramatizing) unrelated to published lesson materials are found in the chapter of Wright, Betteridge, and Buckby (1984) that has to do with magic tricks. The procedure for the "Witness" game in the same book (p. 150) illustrates option 15c (using students' previously existing resources).

The superiority of student-generated images over images supplied by teacher or experimenter was noted by P. R. Stevick (1923: 23) and receives experimental verification in Dickel and Slak (1983: 124).

5 A beginners' textbook

Odyssey, published by Longman in 1983, was adapted by Victoria Kimbrough, Michael Palmer, and Donn Byrne from the British course *Track*. It is a set of materials designed to take secondary school students from the beginning level to high intermediate. It consists of six student books, each accompanied by a workbook, a teacher's manual, and audio recordings. Like many courses down through the years, it uses a structural syllabus, which is to say that it is built around a series of grammatical points. Unlike most such courses, however, it emphasizes both oral communication (as that term was used in exercise 2.1) and reading for information.

There are at least five respects in which *Odyssey* should be effective in the creation and management of mental imagery:
1. Odd-numbered lessons supply scientific or historical information which is interesting in its own right.
2. Even-numbered lessons carry forward a simple continued story about people with whom secondary students are likely to identify.
3. Objects frequently carry strong esthetic and emotional associations: a dolphin (Unit 1) instead of the usual book or other trite object, for example, or (Unit 8) a chimpanzee as a pet instead of a dog or cat.
4. Illustrations are from a number of artists, in a number of styles, thus preserving a freshness that would almost certainly have been lost by any one artist no matter how skilled.
5. Each unit begins with preparatory activities. One of these is talk about the subject matter, either in the target language (English) or in the students' native language, which refreshes whatever nonverbal imagery the students have that will fit with the new verbal items about to be introduced. Another is the assignment of a listening goal – telling students what *information*, not just what words or what grammatical patterns, to listen for in the new material.

One of the strong features of *Odyssey* is the Teacher's Manual, which is both clear and exceptionally comprehensive, and which is therefore well worth study in its own right. In this chapter we will look only at the first unit in Book 1 and at some of the options that are available with it. The first two pages that the student uses are reproduced in Figure 5.1 (pp. 82–3).

Needless to say, no teacher's manual can list all of the possible variations of technique; there simply would not be enough space, and even if there were, the result would be so long and complex that it would fail to give the clear, firm guidance that many teachers need. The writers of such a manual have to hope that users of their course will bring their own skills and ingenuity to bear on the task of teaching. The purpose of this chapter is to help you develop such skills and to encourage you to practice exercising that kind of ingenuity.

Exercise 5.1

The instructions to the teacher begin as follows:

In each unit, suggestions are given for teaching certain structural and vocabulary items that are necessary for a complete understanding of the material. You may wish to teach them before you present the text or dialog, or you may prefer to let the students listen to or read the material first and get the general idea before analyzing any new items. [Teacher's Manual to Book 1, p. vii]

1. What are the advantages and disadvantages of each of the two courses of action described here?
2. What does each alternative imply with regard to mental imagery?

COMMENTS

The paragraph quoted at the beginning of this exercise contains a new option:

OPTION 16: WHETHER TO PRE-TEACH FORMS

a. Present selected new words or grammatical features one at a time, with explanation through simple demonstration or through the native language, before they appear in a full-scale meaningful context. Such a full-scale context may take any of a number of forms: a dialog, or a reading passage, or a radio newscast, or a foreign movie, for example. New verbal images – words and phrases – are being assembled in anticipation of the early arrival of nonverbal items with which they will fit. Advantages: (i) Doing so may forestall anxiety or annoyance on the part of some students. (ii) The full-scale context will be more meaningful to students the first time they hear it, and for some types of context the first time may also be the last.
b. Students meet new words or structures for the first time in the full-scale context. Advantages: (i) These circumstances require the student to practice the kind of attention which is necessary in everyday use of language – noticing new verbal items and the nonverbal items that are associated with them, but not stopping to clutch at every unfa-

miliar word. (ii) Without a certain amount of this kind of experience, students may persist in the belief that they cannot learn new things unless those new things are explicitly taught to them.

Exercise 5.2

The authors' instructions for presenting the text on page 2 of *Odyssey* (see Figure 5.1 on pp. 82–3) are:
a. Ask the students to cover up the text. Explain that they will have a chance to look at it again later.
b. Play the tape of the text or read the text aloud. The students simultaneously listen and look at the illustrations.
c. Ask for the answers to focus questions. (For p. 2, the focus question is "Which of these animals are fish?")
d. Repeat (b), this time with students looking at the printed text as they listen.
e. Have students read silently.
f. Discuss language difficulties (as described elsewhere in the teacher's manual).
g. Work on pronunciation (as described elsewhere).
h. Repeat (b) as a final review, with students' books open or closed.

1. Which alternatives does this procedure specify from options 1–15 (see list in appendix)?
2. To what extent do you think that other alternatives from those same options would also work with this activity?
3. Which others of options 1–15 might be exercised in presenting the material shown in Figure 5.1?

COMMENTS

Options 3 (choral vs. individual response), 4 (order of student response), 5 (calling on students), and 6 (moving through the materials) are all available briefly in step (c). You might even conceivably try option 2b (pause before student response), though I doubt it would be worthwhile here. This procedure calls for alternative (b) of option 10: Begin with an option that you think will challenge students without discouraging or hopelessly confusing them. Ask students to begin without the help of the printed word. Even if they know no English at all, this is not really dangerous. The amount of language to which they are exposed here, and the amount of time before they see the sentences in the book, are both sufficiently short so that few students are likely to worry.

This procedure exemplifies a further choice that is very frequently available to language teachers.

OPTION 17: HEARING BEFORE READING?

a. Students are allowed to follow in their books as they listen to the sentences for the first time. Advantages: (i) This is traditionally the most common alternative, and so requires less effort from both teacher and students. (ii) It is less likely to produce anxiety among the "eye-minded" members of the class.

b. Reading is postponed until after the students have heard the material one or more times, and perhaps until after they have produced it orally themselves. (This was *de rigeur* in the Oral Approach, which dominated 20 years of language teaching in the United States.) Advantages: (i) Students' ears have a chance to hear the words as they are actually pronounced, without influence from prior associations with printed letters. (ii) This alternative allows and requires students to practice a kind of attention which is close to what they need for language outside the classroom.

FURTHER COMMENTS ON EXERCISE 5.2

The procedure also calls for alternative (a) from option 8: All of the initiative is in the hands of the teacher. But isn't this alternative inescapable if the students are really beginners? Not necessarily. Your group may be able to think of ways for starting out with option 8b (student initiative).

Here is one technique for starting page 2 of *Odyssey* using student initiative (option 8b):

a. The lesson plan in the Teacher's Manual calls for the teacher to begin the lesson by giving one or more focus questions, generally in the students' language, to guide their listening. For Unit 1, the focus question is "Which of these animals are fish?" After posing this question, the teacher continues by asking the students to suggest (in their language) two or three questions that they could use in getting that kind of information about the animals in the pictures. The teacher gives them the target-language sentences that correspond to these questions: "Is this a fish?" or "What kind of animal is this?" for example.

b. Students point to the pictures on page 2 and ask the questions *in either language*. No matter which language a student has chosen to use, the teacher repeats the question in the target language and then

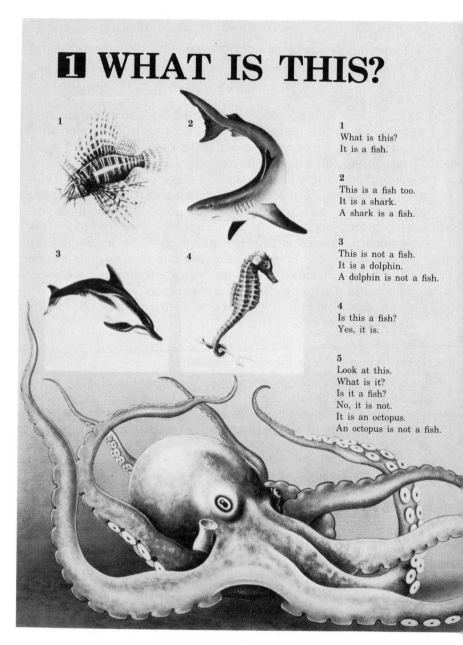

1 WHAT IS THIS?

1
What is this?
It is a fish.

2
This is a fish too.
It is a shark.
A shark is a fish.

3
This is not a fish.
It is a dolphin.
A dolphin is not a fish.

4
Is this a fish?
Yes, it is.

5
Look at this.
What is it?
Is it a fish?
No, it is not.
It is an octopus.
An octopus is not a fish.

Figure 5.1. Pages 2–3 from Unit 1 in *Odyssey*, Student's Book 1, by Victoria Kimbrough, Michael Palmer, and Donn Byrne. The pages have been converted to black and white and reduced in size for reproduction here. (Reproduced with permission. © 1983 by Longman.)

Grammar

This	is	a fish.
	is not isn't	an octopus.

Is	this	a fish?		Yes, it is.	
			No, it	is not. isn't.	
What is What's	this?			It is It's	a fish.

DO YOU UNDERSTAND?

1 Answer *yes* **or** *no*:

PICTURE ONE
Is this a fish?

PICTURE TWO
Is this a fish?

PICTURE THREE
Is this a fish?

PICTURE FOUR
Is this a dolphin?
Is it a fish?

PICTURE FIVE
Is this an octopus?
Is it a fish?

2 Right or wrong?

a. A shark is a fish.
b. A dolphin isn't a fish.
c. An octopus is a fish.

1 Point to the pictures.
Make true sentences:

This	is isn't	a fish. a shark. a dolphin. an octopus.

2 Point to the pictures.
Ask and answer the questions:

a.
S1: What's this?
S2: It's *a dolphin/an octopus.*

b.
S1: Is this *a fish?*
S2: Yes, it is./No, it isn't.

three 3

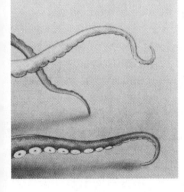

Figure 5.1 (cont.)

83

answers it in the target language. The students' use of the target language is not corrected at this time.

c. Students continue to ask the questions, this time entirely in the target language. The teacher replies, sometimes making errors of fact (option 13b).

These three steps are derived from one of the most successful techniques of Counseling-Learning, an approach developed by Charles A. Curran. Nevertheless, adoption of this procedure does not in itself constitute use of Counseling-Learning, since it does not provide for systematic understanding of the students' reactions. Options 6 (moving through the materials) and 14 (use of teacher's voice) are simple options, but through skillful shifting among their alternatives as we follow the procedure suggested in the Teacher's Manual, we can allow students to get additional listening practice without making them feel that they are just doing the same thing over and over.

Exercise 5.3

The next activity, "Do You Understand?" on page 3 of *Odyssey*, requires students to understand questions and to reply with simple *yes/no* answers. The procedure given in the Teacher's Manual is:

a. Read the question aloud. Address the whole class to involve all the students. In some cases you may have to hold up the book and point to a picture while reading the question.

b. Ask for volunteers.

c. Choose a student to answer.

d. Confirm or correct the answer or ask another student to do this.

e. Arrange the students in pairs for further practice on their own.

1. Which alternatives does this procedure specify from options 1–17 (see appendix)?

2. To what extent to you think that other alternatives from those same options would also work with this activity?

3. Which others of options 1–17 might be exercised in presenting the material shown on page 3?

COMMENTS

The above procedure rather clearly calls for options 3b (students respond individually) and 8a (teacher takes the initiative). Most teachers would instinctively have students respond immediately here (option 2a). Option 5 (calling on students) is available on a small scale. Options 6 (moving through the materials) and 14 (use of teacher's voice) are again of potential value, as they were in exercise 5.2. Step (b) adds a new alternative to option 4: allowing students to volunteer answers. The advantage of this alternative is that students who are not ready to answer are not put on the spot.

Step (d) implies another set of choices which every language teacher faces many times a day:

OPTION 18: HOW TO RESPOND TO ERRORS OF LANGUAGE

a. Ignore errors entirely. Advantages: (i) This saves time and makes the class go more smoothly. (ii) It doesn't remind the students of their "ignorant, powerless and constantly evaluated" status (Stevick 1982: 10), and so allows them to feel that they are engaged in restricted but genuine use of the language. Storing this kind of emotional item along with the verbal items will make the verbal items more easily available in the future.

b. Give direct corrections. For example, respond to an answer of "djess" by immediately presenting the correct pronunciation "yes" and having the student repeat it after you. You may present the new model in a stern voice, or cordially, or in a neutral tone, and each of these three has its own advantages and disadvantages. The overall advantage of this alternative is that the student finds out immediately where the error is, and has a chance to improve by repeating after you. Using this alternative too often, however, no matter what tone of voice you use, can leave the student with the impression that the main purpose of speaking a foreign language is to avoid the need for correction, and may lead to lathophobic aphasia – the inability to speak for fear of making a mistake.

c. Pretend you haven't understood. For example, say, " 'Djess'?" The student tries again. If the second attempt produces "yes," you indicate that you have understood and go on with the next sentence. If it still produces an error, you finally "understand": "Oh! 'Yes!' " Advantages: (i) This keeps students from becoming prematurely satisfied with their own imperfect productions, and thus reduces the chance that they will form unsatisfactory permanent habits. (ii) It maintains the feeling of a conversation in which two people are trying to communicate with each other. The difficulty is that it quickly develops a credibility gap, because students know that, for example, "djess" is clearly not "no." Since "yes" and "no" were the only available answers, the teacher must really have known what the student meant the first time.

d. Repeat the word or sentence correctly somewhere in whatever you say next. Student: "Djess." Teacher: "Yes! Yes, it *is* a fish!" Advantages: (i) A conversational tone is maintained, while at the same time allowing the class to hear the correct form. (ii) There is no danger of a credibility gap. (iii) This way of responding to errors allows students to hear some of the ways in which native speakers repeat and confirm information in ordinary conversation.

But teachers need to do more than look at the *errors* that their students make. They must also have alternative ways of responding to what they do *right*.

e. The most common way of dealing with a correct response, I suppose, is to say something like "Right!" or "Very good!" and to give the student an encouraging smile. The advantages of this alternative are that this sort of response is explicit and that many students respond positively to a certain amount of it. The disadvantage is that if used often, it can quickly come to appear perfunctory, insincere, and even condescending. It also takes class time and breaks up concentration on what is being studied.

f. Another way of dealing with correct responses is to explain that what a student has said will receive no comment unless there is something about it which calls for more work to be done. This is the convention that is used in the Silent Way, and it can work quite well. The disadvantage is that it is different from what most students have come to expect, and so may take some getting used to. Whether one uses (e) or (f), however, I have concluded from my own experience both as student and as teacher that the teacher's *nonverbal* expressions of *pleasure* are safer, less time-consuming, and more constructive than *verbal* expressions of *approval*.

Step e of the procedure on page 84 is one side of another important choice:

OPTION 19: WITH WHOM SHOULD THE STUDENTS TALK?

a. Students question and answer each other. Advantages: (i) They have a chance to do more speaking per hour than if they talked only with the teacher. (ii) They have an opportunity to speak without feeling that they are the objects of the teacher's critical attention. There are a few real dangers in this alternative, however. One is that it easily becomes perfunctory and dull – a mere mechanical manipulation of words. A second is that the pace of the activity may drag. The most obvious, but in my opinion the least serious, is that students may unintentionally practice errors which are not immediately detected by the teacher.

b. Students question the teacher. This of course works well with option 8b (students take the initiative). The students know pretty much what the substance of the answer is going to be, but the teacher can clothe this substance in a great variety of linguistic forms. We saw an example of this in exercise 4.15:

Yes! It is a *fish*!

Yes! It *is* a fish!
Yes, it's a fish.
Yes, it is.
Yes!
The teacher can also hide words, as in options 9b and c:
This one here? Oh, yes, it's a fish!
A fish, you say? Yes, it's a fish.
[*in a surprised tone*] Yeah! It *is* a *fish*! It's a fish, all right!
etc.
Advantages: (i) Students get the satisfaction of feeling that they have initiated a brief conversation in which the other person has a lively interest. (This kind of thing may look as though it should produce a credibility gap, but in my experience it does not.) (ii) Students get to hear the language of real conversation, yet with no difficulty in understanding the message and with no feeling that they are responsible for reproducing the full range of language at this stage. This is actually an application of alternatives (b) and (c) from option 9. (iii) The pace of the activity doesn't drag.

Exercise 5.4

The two shaded blocks in the upper right corner of page 3 (Figure 5.1) are a simple and very common way of presenting grammar. The purpose of such a block is to make graphic the relationships among the parts of a number of sentences which have the same surface structure: sentences such as "This is a fish," "This is not an octopus," "This isn't a dolphin." The tabular format makes it easier for students to see what kinds of words go where, and what combinations of words are and are not permitted. Some students can learn from a substitution table just by looking at it. Others are more likely to profit from it if they do a simple drill with it, as suggested in the Teacher's Manual (p. ix):
T [pointing to picture in book]: This is a fish. Shark.
S1 [pointing to picture]: This is a shark.
T: Octopus.
[etc.]

1. What possible value can there be in this kind of activity?
2. What options can you find for it?

COMMENTS

This kind of drill was a standby of one variety of the Oral Approach. It has fallen into disfavor with many language teachers these days because it tends to become a mere manipulation of words, with no assurance that appropriate nonverbal items are being stored along with the verbal ones. The directions for the drill quoted here partly avoid that danger by requiring students and teacher alike to point to pictures as they speak. It seems to me that there is still a place for this kind of drill if it is recognized for what it is: an exploration of the regularities – the patterns – within verbal imagery in the new language, but not practice of the language itself. The alternatives from option 2 (timing of student responses) are available here.

Exercise 5.5

The next activity on page 3 of *Odyssey* is based on the unshaded box. The teacher is instructed to "call on one student at a time to hold up his/her book, point to a picture, and make a sentence about it."

1. How does imagery figure in this kind of activity?
2. What are some of the options?

COMMENTS

Asking a student to make a sentence using some specific word or some specific tense or other grammatical form is an ancient technique. It requires the student not only to generate words, but also to decide on some kind of nonverbal items which are to be expressed by those words. This never happens in language use outside the classroom, of course, and so it is artificially difficult for any student. Even when one student comes up with a nonverbal image and manages to express it in correct language, the nonverbal image is unlikely to have any connections with other nonverbal imagery present in the minds of the other students. Purposive items are particularly likely to be trivial. For these reasons, both the meaning and the linguistic form are likely to get lost in memory. Again, as in exercise 5.4, the writers of the Teacher's Manual partially avoid this pitfall by having people point to pictures.

Option 4 (order of student response) is obviously available here. This activity also provides yet another pair of options:

OPTION 20: SINGLE OR MULTIPLE USE

a. As suggested in the Teacher's Manual, have each student make one sentence and point to one picture. Advantage: The activity takes a relatively small amount of time.
b. Once a student has come up with a sentence that is true for a picture, have the same student or other students use the same sentence with other pictures for which it is also true. For example, "This isn't an

octopus" can go with four out of the five pictures, and "This is a fish" can go with three. Advantages: (i) Students experience the meaning of each sentence more fully. (ii) They get more practice and a greater return on the investment that was required in order to select a sentence in the first place and to assemble the logogens needed in order to produce it.

Options 16–20 have been concerned with choices that are available from within the materials as published. Under many circumstances, it is wise to stay as close as possible to what is in print. Occasionally, however, you may want to go beyond the book.

SUPER OPTION 21: WHETHER TO SUPPLEMENT THE PRINTED MATERIALS

a. Stick with what is in the book. Advantages: (i) It takes less of your valuable time and energy. (ii) It is less likely to be confusing to your students. (iii) If your students are going to be taught later by other teachers in the same program, your class will fit more easily with the classes of your colleagues.
b. Supplement the book. Advantages: (i) Students get to meet the same grammar or vocabulary in a new context and from a different perspective. (ii) The change of pace may be refreshing both to you and to the students. (iii) Not least, your ideas may turn out to be very successful.

Exercise 5.6

There is much talk these days within the language teaching profession about the advantages of allowing students to have a long "silent period," during which they hear great quantities of meaningful and comprehensible language without having to do more than respond with actions or with very simple words. One version of this approach does not allow students to do even that. They just listen as two native speakers talk with each other, animatedly and with various purposes. Of course, the talk must be intelligible to the students, either because it uses words they know or because it is about objects and actions that they can watch. Any new words must be used many times before the teacher can feel safe in depending on them, and this means that there can be no more than a very few words "pending" at any one time.

The following is a possible introduction to Unit 1 of *Odyssey*, or to early lessons in many other structural syllabuses, based on those principles. Because few classrooms have two native speakers in them, I have adapted the idea for solo voice. (The symbol + indicates the first occurrence of a word.)

Mostly about options

1. Try reading the monolog aloud as it stands, perhaps to the other members of your group.
2. What general strengths and weaknesses do you find in it?
3. If you were going to use this monolog with a class, what small changes in wording would you make? Compare your answers with the answers of the other members of your group.

Sample of an animated monolog

leaf	+Leaf ... leaf ... *(thoughtfully)* ... leaf? ... *(as with a flash*
a	*of insight)* ... Leaf! ... + A leaf! ... *(Draws leaf on board.)*
aha, this, is	+ Aha! ... A leaf! ... *(triumphantly)* ... + This + *is* a leaf!
yes, it	... *(softly, thoughtfully)* + Yes, this is ... Yes, + it *is* a leaf!
	... *(looks down, as if deciding what to do next. Then looks*
feather	*up, as if with a sudden inspiration.)* A + feather! ... A
	feather! ...
Hmm	+ Hmm! ... A feather! ... *(Draws feather on board.)*
and	+ And *this* ... *(pointing)* ... *this* ... *(pointing again, em-*
	phatically) is a feather! ... A feather? ... *(Looks back and*
	forth between picture of feather and real feather.) ... *(in*
	a pleased tone)
that	Yes, a feather! ... *This (pointing)* is a feather, ... and + *that*
	(pointing) is a leaf! ... *(sounding very self-satisfied)* Yes, a
	leaf and a feather! ... A feather and a leaf! ... *That (point-*
	ing) is a feather, and *this (pointing)* is a leaf! *This* is a leaf,
	and that *(slowing down)* is ... a ... feather!
	(Draws dollar or local banknote on board.)
	(quickly, excitedly) And this! ... Aha! ... *This (pointing)* is
dollar	a + dollar! ... A dollar! ... *(pointing rapidly from one pic-*
	ture to another) A dollar, a feather, a leaf! ... A leaf, a
	feather, a dollar! ... A feather, a dollar, a *(sudden slow-*
	down, voice drops to quiet, conspiratorial tone) ... a leaf!
	(As if with sudden realization that something is wrong)
wait, real	+ Wait! ... *(pointing)* ... Is this a leaf? ... A + *real* leaf?
no, picture,	... + No! ... No, this is a + picture + of a leaf! ... A pic-
of	ture! ... *This (pointing)* is a picture ... a picture ... a pic-
	ture *of* a leaf, and that ... *that (pointing)* is a real leaf! ...
	(more rapidly, as if having just caught on) ... And that is
	a real feather, and this is a *picture* of ... a picture *of* a
	feather, and that is a real dollar, and this is a picture of a
	dollar! *(with evident satisfaction)* Yes! This *(pointing to*
	one picture) is a picture, and that *(pointing)* is real, and
	this *(pointing to second picture)* is a picture, and that
	(pointing) is real, and that *(pointing)* is real, and this *(slow-*
	ing down) ... is ... a ... picture! *(triumphantly)* Mm-hmm!

(Moves toward the objects and away from the board.) This *(grasping, shaking, feeling feather)* is a real feather, and that *(pointing)* is a picture ... a picture of a leaf. This *(waving money in air)* is real! It's a real dollar! ... And that *(pointing)* ... that's a picture of a dollar.

(Pauses to take stock of what he or she has learned, then begins to reiterate it once more.) That (pointing) is + not a real dollar. No, that is *not* a real dollar. This *(waving)* is a real dollar. This *is* real, and that *(pointing)* isn't. It isn't real. That isn't a real dollar, + but this *(waving)* is. It is a real dollar. *(as if with new realization)* And this *(grasping)* is a real leaf, but that *(pointing)* is a picture of a leaf. It's a picture. And that's a picture, + too! It isn't a real feather. It's a *picture* of a feather! *This* is a real feather! *That* is a picture ... a *picture* of a feather!

+ Now! *(Puts feather and leaf and dollar into a large bag which already contains a copy of the textbook. Gropes around in it with eyes closed.)* Now! + *What* ... what is this? Is it a dollar? Is it a feather? *(Withdraws feather.)* Aha! It's a feather! Yes, it is. It's a feather. It's not a dollar. *(Shakes head.)* No, it isn't. It's a feather! *(Replaces feather in bag and continues groping.)* Now, what ... what is this? A dollar? ... A feather? ... *(Withdraws dollar.)* Aha! It's a dollar! + It is not a feather. No, it isn't. It isn't a feather! It's a dollar. Yes, it is! ... *(Replaces dollar in bag and continues groping.)* Now, what is this? *(Frowns.)* It's not a dollar. No, it isn't. No, it's not a dollar, and it's not a feather. No, it isn't a feather. What is it? *(Withdraws the textbook.)* It's a + book! ... A book! ... A real book! *(Opens book and points to picture of shark.)* And this ... this is a picture. *(Laughs.)* A real picture! It's a picture of a + fish. And this *(pointing to seahorse)* is a picture of a fish, too! *This* fish *(pointing to shark)* is a ... *(voice shifts to ominous tone)* a + shark. *(gesture of sudden, savage biting)* A shark is a fish. And this *(pointing, voice smaller and daintier)* is a + seahorse *(voice normal)* A seahorse is a fish, too.

not

but

too

now!

what

book

fish

shark

seahorse

COMMENTS

This technique makes full use of options 12b (dramatizing) and 14a, b (use of the teacher's voice). It also works with 15a (beginning by assuming students cannot produce/comprehend). The teacher's wrong guesses while groping in the bag are examples of option 13b (making factual errors).

guesses while groping in the bag are examples of option 13b (making factual errors).

When first written, this monolog had *book* and *chair* in place of *leaf* and *feather*. The original words were more generally useful to beginning learners of a language, but I changed words because *book* and *chair* are so trite and classroomy, and because *leaf* and *feather* have something to do with living things. These are two of three domains from which we may draw nonverbal imagery:

What is normally at hand: objects and activities in the classroom

What is interesting in itself: dolphins, dollars, anecdotes, games, curios, etc.

What is of foreseeable use to the learners: ordering a meal in a restaurant, filling out an application for employment, bricklaying, etc.

Summary

The format of *Odyssey* is quite different from the format of *Before Book One*, and somewhat more familiar. Yet virtually all of the options developed in Chapter 4 have reappeared in Chapter 5. Of the new options in Chapter 5, only one (whether or not to have students listen to a sample of language before they see it printed) is concerned only with language. Two of the others (how to react to errors, and whom students should talk with) deal primarily with social relationships within the classroom. The others (whether or not to pre-teach, whether or not to make multiple use of sentences, and whether to supplement the printed materials) are concerned with the stuff of straight pedagogy: the economical use of time and other resources, the maintenance of some sort of rhythm in classroom activity, and the concurrent production of verbal and nonverbal imagery.

We have looked at only the first two of the six pages of the first unit of the first book in a 6-volume series, and so we have hardly done justice to the resources which *Odyssey* offers to teachers and learners of English. We have, however, added to our range of experience of what can be done with a lesson when we look for options, and when we evaluate the alternatives in terms of verbal and nonverbal imagery.

In the literature

Vigil and Oller (1976) is an important article on the ways in which feedback from native speakers may either promote or prevent the premature fossilization of students' language. The effects of various styles of correction by the teacher are discussed by Gerngross and Puchta (1984: 97, 104) and by Raimes (1983: 150).

Several other options for use with mechanical drills of this general type are found in Chapters 8–10 of Stevick (1982) and will not be repeated here.

For information about Counseling-Learning, see Curran (1976) and Part 3 of Stevick (1980).

The animated monolog is based on ideas found in Asher (1982) and Krashen and Terrell (1983) and modified by Adrian Palmer and J. Marvin Brown. The either "absent-minded" or "emphatic" repetition of words in the sample monolog in exercise 5.6 receives some support from research reported by Chaudron (1983).

6 An intermediate textbook

Transitions is an intermediate-level textbook by Linda Ferreira (Newbury House, 1984). It is the second in a three-part series titled *Express English* by the same author.

The table of contents of this book contains three columns. The first column is headed "Scene" and tells what is going on among the fictional characters in each lesson. The second column, "Practice," lists the grammar points that receive special attention in the lesson. The last column is "Expression" and contains functional items as that term was used in exercise 2.2: refusing an invitation, agreeing and disagreeing tactfully, and so forth.

Transitions has at least two very conspicuous strengths. One is that, like the books that we looked at in Chapters 4 and 5, it is blessed with a very clear and thorough Teacher's Manual. The other is that the 24 lessons develop a single story about a small set of interesting people, complete with character, conflict, and romance. The size and complexity of this story should allow students to form much fuller nonverbal images with any given sentence than they would be able to form from the same sentence if they met it in a grammar drill, or even in the context of a single interesting anecdote.

The "Uptown" section of Unit 2

The "Uptown" section of Unit 2 in the Student's Book is reproduced in Figure 6.1. The Teacher's Manual suggests the following basic procedure for use with the narration and dialog on this page:

a. Read to the students the following synopsis:

> Preston Wade is Susan's father. His business headquarters is on Park Avenue in Manhattan. He's a wealthy and powerful man. Wade owns a construction company. His dream is to build Wade Plaza. He's looking at the architect's plans with his assistant, Kemp.

Students cover the printed matter while the synopsis is being read.

b. Students read the opening caption:

Preston Wade started his construction company 30 years ago. He's going to build Wade Plaza this year.

As they look at the pictures, the teacher asks:

When did Wade start his company?
What does Wade's company do?
What is Wade's dream?

c. Write on the board the following questions:

How did Wade make his first million?
What is Wade's new project?
What problem are they discussing?

d. Play the tape of this scene once through without stopping. Students look at the picture, but not at the print.

e. Write on the board:

has a lot of ambition
used the profits
It's a cooperative.
You can count on me.

Repeat these several times with the students, and explain any expressions that are unfamiliar to them.

f. Play the tape a second time. You may or may not want to stop it at points where students have difficulty, but don't stop to explain the meaning of all of the new vocabulary.

g. Play the tape through a third time, without stopping. At this time, or if there is a fourth playing, students may follow the text in their books.

h. Read "Questions." The teacher may begin the questioning, or may call on individual students to question and answer each other.

i. Discuss with the students:

Are there business and shopping plazas in your country?
Can you buy apartments in your country?
Do people buy a building and form a cooperative?

Exercise 6.1

1. For which among options 1–21 (see appendix) are the alternatives already specified in step (a) of the preceding procedure?
2. Which others of options 1–21 are available in step (a)?
3. Give examples of how the options you selected in (2) could be applied to page 8 (Figure 6.1).

Mostly about options

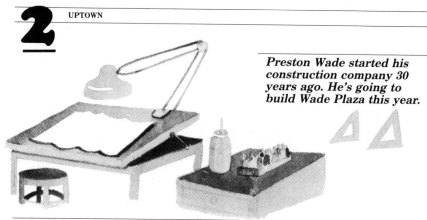

2 UPTOWN

Preston Wade started his construction company 30 years ago. He's going to build Wade Plaza this year.

Scene One

🔊 Thirty-five years ago, Preston Wade came to New York and got a job as a builder. He didn't have much money then, but he had a lot of ambition. He soon learned all about the construction business. With his savings, Wade bought some equipment and hired a few men. He had his own company only a year when he made his first million dollars.

Wade used the profits from his construction company to buy property in Manhattan. Ten years ago he built the Wade Building on Park Avenue as his business headquarters. By that time, Wade was a wealthy and powerful man.

Last year Wade began to buy property on Manhattan's West Side. He hired a famous architect to design the plans for Wade Plaza, a new group of luxury apartments, boutiques, shops, and restaurants. At 66, Wade was a man with a dream. He wanted the people of New York to look at Wade Plaza, its beauty and its power. Wade wanted them to remember him long after his death.

As usual, Preston Wade was in his office in the Wade Building by 8:00 A.M.. Kemp, his assistant, wanted Wade to look at a section of the plans for Wade Plaza. Kemp was an impatient man. He wanted Wade to make a decision.

KEMP Well, what do you think?
WADE These plans look complete. Are we ready to build?
KEMP Not yet. There's one problem. Wade Enterprises owns all the land except this corner property here, the section next to the park.
WADE Let me see those plans again. What's there now?
KEMP Tudor Village, an old apartment house. It's a cooperative. All the tenants own the building and they don't want to leave.
WADE Buy them out, Kemp. That's your job.
KEMP Yeah, sure. I can get them out of there.
WADE You do that, Kemp. It's your problem now.
KEMP Right. You can count on me.

8

Questions

Ask and answer:
1 if Preston Wade got his first job in business or in construction. When?
Question Did Preston Wade get his first job in business or in construction?
Answer He got his first job in construction.
Question When did Wade get his first job?
Answer Thirty-five years ago, when he came to New York.
2 if Wade was lucky or clever in those early years. How?
Question Was Wade lucky or clever in those early years?
Answer He was clever in those early years.
Question How was Wade clever?
Answer He worked hard and saved his money.
3 if Wade built the Wade Building or Wade Plaza ten years ago.
4 if Wade is going to build an office building or a plaza complex this year. Where? Why?
5 if Wade needs to buy the park or the Tudor Village property. Why?
6 if Tudor Village is Wade's or Kemp's problem. Why?

Figure 6.1. Page 8 from Unit 2 in *Transitions*, Student's Book, by Linda Ferreira. The material has been converted to black and white and reduced in size for reproduction here. (Reproduced with permission. © 1984 by Newbury House Publishers.)

COMMENTS

The procedure given in the Teacher's Manual clearly calls for option 8a (teacher initiative) and 17b (hearing before reading). In addition, the use of a brief synopsis, instead of plunging students directly into the entire recording of scene one, is a form of 16a (pre-teaching). It is also consistent with 15b, in that it assumes that students can understand most of the synopsis but are not yet ready to speak on their own. And it seems to take option 20a (using material in only one way), with the teacher reading the synopsis only once, and reading it only in the form in which it is printed.

Two options for which the alternatives are not specified are 12 (dramatizing) and 14 (use of teacher's voice). Reading aloud, if we are to take literally the words of the manual, is in my experience almost always done in a firm, clear, deliberate voice – options 12a and 14a. This kind of reading transmits two messages to the ears of the students. One, of course, is the words.

The other message is confirmation that the relationship between speaker and hearers is that of teacher and pupils, and that the purpose of the activity is to hear and remember language. In the short run, this makes the class go smoothly. I sometimes wonder, however, whether the classroomish emotional and purposive items that are stored in memory along with the words may also produce an underdifferentiated experience which in the long run will turn out to be relatively sterile.

Exercise 6.2

1. Try reading the synopsis under item (a) (p. 94) using the customary clear, deliberate "teacher voice."
2. Read the same synopsis in some other way. Let the other members of your group comment on the differences between your two readings.

COMMENTS

A teacher who chose alternatives 12b (putting the material into a brief role play) and 14b (speaking in a normal, relaxed voice) or even 14c (dramatizing in a normal or rapid voice) might *say* to the students something like this:

Now, I want to tell you a little about scene 1. There are two people in it. One of the two people is Preston Wade. Do you remember Susan Wade in Unit 1? Well, Preston Wade is her father. He owns a construction company ...a construction company, and the headquarters...the headquarters of his company is on Park Avenue – that's in Manhattan. He's really a very wealthy and powerful man. He's very wealthy and powerful, but there is still one thing that he wants. He has a dream – a dream of building something... something that he wants to call "Wade Plaza." (We'll find out what that is when we listen to the tape.) So anyway, in this scene Preston Wade is in his office with his assistant, whose name is Kemp, and he and Kemp are looking at some plans... some plans that an architect has drawn for Wade Plaza.

This sort of monolog adds nothing important either to the ideas or to the vocabulary of the printed synopsis, and it does take a little more time. Then why bother with it? From the point of view of mental imagery, there are at least three reasons: (i) Its very first sentence states a communicative purpose: "I want to tell you something." The *style* of oral delivery should reiterate this message *in every sentence*. (ii) The monolog also contains some of the flags which native speakers commonly use when they are trying to put information across:

"Now..."
"Do you remember...?"
"Well,..."
"So anyway..."

Repetition of parts of sentences.

These flags arc small but important items on the verbal side of the experience. (iii) When students feel that a person is talking to them, rather than that a teacher is reading to them, I suspect that they will become more actively involved in the exchange, and so generate richer nonverbal imagery in their own minds in response to the words that are coming to them through the air.

There are of course disadvantages to this combination of 12b and 14b/c. (i) It requires a bit more class time. (ii) Although it can be (and probably should be) done impromptu, it still requires a bit more preparation on the part of the teacher. (iii) It may be too difficult for some teachers who are not native speakers of the target language. So it is quite possible that, for a manual which must work for the largest number of teachers, the author was right in her choice of options in step (a).

Exercise 6.3

1. For which of options 1–21 (see list in appendix) are the alternatives already specified in step (b) on page 94?
2. Which other options are available in step (b)?
3. Give examples of how the options you selected in (2) could be applied to page 8 of *Transitions* (see Figure 6.1).

COMMENTS

The procedure does not specify whether students are to read the caption at the top of page 8 (Figure 6.1) silently or aloud. In either case, we have literally an example of option 17a (hearing while reading), since the students have not heard these two sentences before. There is little risk here, though, since any difficult words have come up in step (a).

The second half of step (b) is an instance of option 8a (teacher initiative), and with it come all of the alternatives in options 2 (timing of student responses), 3 (choral vs. individual response), 4 (order of student response), 5 (calling on students), 10 (moving from hard to easy or vice versa), and (if students have any trouble in answering) 18 (responding to errors of language). The author apparently intends – wisely, I think – that this step should take only a minute or so, but there is also the possibility of using these three questions in more than one way (20b): (i) Teacher reads the questions from the book in a manner which implies, "Now listen to these questions and see if you can answer them without any errors either of fact or of language." (This is the teacher-student style that I mentioned in the comments on step (a).) (ii) Teacher closes the book, looks absentminded, and asks the same questions as if requesting help in remembering. Again, we have the person-to-person style described in the comments on (a), employing new alternatives in options 12 (dramatizing) and 14 (use of teacher's voice). Here is an opportunity for 9b (hiding the relevant message in longer, more idiomatic sentences) as well: "And Wade's company, what kind of company is it?" "Did you say Wade's company buys and sells buildings?" "Hey, wait a minute! What does the book say about Wade's company?" and so forth. The students don't have to come up with new answers, but they are exposed to many verbal items that native speakers use when they are trying to get help of this kind.

Exercise 6.4

Steps (c)–(g) in the basic procedure (p. 95) represent one alternative in an additional option:

OPTION 22: WHETHER THE STUDENTS SHOULD REPRODUCE EXACTLY THE LANGUAGE THAT IS GIVEN IN THE SAMPLE

a. Students are asked to read the narrative aloud, perhaps one sentence to a student, and then to read the two roles in the dialog portion. Or they repeat it aloud after the tape or the teacher. Advantages: (i) This is what most students and teachers are used to, and so it may be reassuring. (ii) It both allows and requires students to focus at least for a moment on each verbal item in the sample. If a student's verbal resources are insufficient to produce the logogens for a usable pronunciation of a word or phrase, there is an opportunity for the teacher to point this out and to provide a model of correct pronunciation. The purposes of some students, to the extent that they are constantly trying to pick up new information that will help them improve, will lead them to use this new model in order to modify one or more of their logogens.

b. Students draw on what they have heard or read in the sample, but in the context of answering questions or engaging in other kinds of exchanges. Advantages: (i) This avoids the purely mechanical reproduction of words which did not originate in any purpose of the students. (ii) It saves time.

1. How might you add option 22a to the procedure given in the Teacher's Manual (steps a–i, pp. 94–5)?
2. Can you imagine classes for which option 22a would be definitely desirable? Definitely undesirable?
3. Should the author have included some provision for students to read the sample aloud or to repeat it after the teacher? Why, or why not? Discuss this within your group.

COMMENTS

Option 8b (having students take initiative) is part of a technique borrowed from Counseling-Learning called the "Human Computer," which allows students to improve their pronunciation without some of the disadvantages of option 22a:

a. Student 1 reads aloud some word or short phrase from the sample. The student may choose this word either because he or she feels safe with it or because he or she is unsure of how to pronounce it. (As students become more comfortable with this technique, they commonly choose the latter.)
b. The teacher repeats the word or phrase correctly, giving no indication of whether the student's pronunciation was right or wrong.
c. Student 1 may or may not choose to repeat the word or phrase after the teacher.
d. Student 1 goes through steps (a)–(c) a second time, with the same word(s) or with different word(s).
e. Each student has an opportunity to go through steps (a)–(d).
f. From time to time, the teacher may make general comments about points that are still causing difficulty for some people, but these comments are not made in reference to identifiable individuals. In my experience, this technique is about as effective as the traditional

"repeat-after-me-so-I-can-correct-you" technique, and it is less time consuming. With regard to verbal imagery, it allows students to focus on points at which they are conscious of having gaps. Nonverbally, the purpose is to find something out rather than to avoid correction.

Exercise 6.5

Step (h) of the procedure in the Teacher's Manual (p. 95) has to do with the "Questions" section of page 8 (Figure 6.1). The questions and sample answers in this section raise two issues that we discussed in exercises 2.5 and 2.6, and that we should now add to our list of numbered options:

OPTION 23: WHETHER QUESTIONS SHOULD ASK FOR ANSWERS THAT ARE TO BE FOUND IN THE SAMPLE TEXT OR FOR STUDENTS' INFERENCES AND INTERPRETATIONS

a. Answers come from the text.
b. Answers require students to draw on the nonverbal imagery which they have derived from the text.
(The advantages of each of these alternatives were discussed in exercise 2.5 and will not be repeated here.)

1. Make up questions of both kinds for this lesson.
2. Compare your questions with the ones written by the other members of your group. From among all these questions, select five of each type.
3. What *criteria* did you come up with to guide you in your selection of questions?

OPTION 24: WHETHER REPLIES SHOULD BE IN COMPLETE SENTENCES OR IN SENTENCE FRAGMENTS

a. Students reply in complete sentences.
b. Students reply in the kinds of sentence fragments that native speakers would be likely to use in answering the same questions outside of a classroom situation.
(Again, the advantages of each choice have already been mentioned in connection with exercise 2.6 and so will not be discussed here.)

1. Write two or more short answers for each of five of the questions that you wrote for option 23.
2. Under what circumstances, if any, would you use options 23b and 24b with page 8 of *Transitions* (see Figure 6.1)?

COMMENTS

It is possible to write interpretation/inference questions which merely ask students to fill in random gaps in the information actually supplied in the story: "What floor is Wade's office on?" and the like. It is also possible to organize such questions. For example, you can use questions of the type "In what ways is he like many other people?" "In what ways is he unusual?" "What do you like about Wade?" "Which do you think are probably true about Preston Wade?"

– He's a very relaxed person.
– He sleeps less than six hours a night.
– He likes to travel.
– He's generous to his friends.
– He's generous to community organizations.
– He likes to go to parties.

"What makes you guess as you do?"

These questions, like random questions, require the students to use language taken from the sample, and then reward them for doing so. They do not allow the students to stop there, however. The students must contribute nonverbal ideas from their own imagination or their own reasoning, and they must supply the words that are necessary in order to put the facts of the story into the framework of the questions. Answers to these questions thus make a long-term contribution to the *non*visual varieties of *non*verbal items which students will attach to future episodes of the story.

Students may of course be given the responsibility of making up such questions (option 8b, student initiative).

The "Practice" section of Unit 2

Figure 6.2 is a reproduction of page 10 in the Student's Book of *Transitions*.

The first grammatical structure that is singled out for practice in Unit 2 is the simple past tense. The Teacher's Manual suggests that the teacher first demonstrate the meaning of the past tense through actions, and then ask past-tense questions to which the students can reply with facts that are true for them: "Were you hungry last night?" "Did you walk to school today?" and the like. Both of these activities ensure a dependable source for appropriate nonverbal items: actions that have just taken place before everyone's eyes, or the experiences of individual students.

2 PRACTICE ONE

Simple Past

| Did | the plane the passengers | arrive | on time? late? | Yes, it did. No, they didn't. |

| Was the plane | late? | No, it wasn't. |
| Were the passengers | on time? | Yes, they were. |

| When did the passengers arrive? | At 10:25. |
| Who arrived at 10:25? | The passengers did. |

We use the **simple past** tense to tell about an action or state that happened or was true at a time in the past. When *who* or *what* is the subject of the sentence, we do not use the *did-pattern* to form a question.

A Tell about the story. Complete these sentences with the *past tense* of regular verbs and *was(n't)* or *were(n't)*.

1 The doctor (telephone) with the news about Kathryn. Wade _____ upset.
2 Kathryn _____ very old. Wade (marry) her when she was 21 years old.
3 Wade (pick) up Kathryn's photograph. He _____ sad.
4 Wade (start) his business with a lot of hard work and a little money. He _____ lazy.
5 Wade _____ clever. He (use) company profits to expand his business.

6 Kemp (wait) for Wade to look over the plans. Kemp _____ impatient.
7 Kemp and Wade (discover) the Tudor Village problem. They _____ happy.
8 Kemp and Wade _____ angry. They (want) to build Wade Plaza soon.

C Read about Kathryn and Preston Wade's wedding and complete the story with the correct form of these verbs.

attend   marry
carry   perform
follow   receive
graduate   serve
leave   wear

Kathryn Davis, New York Heiress, Weds

Kathryn Gayle Davis _____ Preston Wade, New York industrialist and president of Wade Enterprises, in Manhattan yesterday. The Reverend Charles Jenkins _____ the ceremony at St. William's Church on Park Avenue. The reception for 300 guests _____ at the Plaza Hotel.

Miss Davis, daughter of John Davis, founder of Davis Department Stores, _____ from Miss Porter's School and _____ Vassar College. The bride, a fashion editor at *Vogue*, _____ a white silk gown with Belgian lace. She _____ a bouquet of roses and orchids.

Mr. Wade _____ on the City Planning Board and _____ the *Good Citizen Award* from the NY City Council last year.

After the reception, Mr. and Mrs. Wade _____ for a two-week trip to Hawaii.

B Make wh-questions with the *past tense* to ask each other about the story.

1 Someone called Wade. Who? When?

S1 Who called Wade?
S2 The doctor did.
S3 When did he call?
S4 At midnight.

2 Someone telephoned the airlines. Who? Why?
3 Something happened to Kathryn. What? When?
4 Someone wanted to own Tudor Village? Who? Why?
5 Something landed at 10:25 this morning. What? Where?

● Make questions to ask each other with *who*, *what*, *where*, and *when* and the past tense of these irregular verbs.

eat/ate	have/had	take/took
buy/bought	go/went	read/read
come/came	make/made	see/saw

1 dinner last night
→ Who had chicken for dinner last night?
→ What did you make for dinner last night?
→ Where did you eat dinner last night?
→ When did you have dinner last night?

2 department store last week
3 school today
4 vacation last year
5 work yesterday
6 television last night
7 breakfast this morning
8 trip last month

Figure 6.2. Page 10 from Unit 2 in *Transitions*, Student's Book, by Linda Ferreira. The material has been converted to black and white and reduced in size for reproduction here. (Reproduced with permission. © 1984 by Newbury House Publishers.)

Exercise 6.6

Activities A and B in Unit 2 are based on scene 2, found on page 9 of the Student's Book of *Transitions*. Page 9, which is not pictured here but is identical in format with page 8 (Figure 6.1), tells about Preston Wade's marriage to Kathryn, who died when their daughter Susan was born. Students have to draw on material from both these scenes in order to do the practice exercises which follow.

The printed instructions in the Teacher's Manual for activity A are: "Read directions, and have students give the simple past of the verb in parentheses and of the verb *to be*. Check for correct pronunciation of past endings."

1. Which of options 1–24 (see list in appendix) are available for activity A?
2. How would you conduct this part of the lesson?

COMMENTS

Presumably the directions mean that the teacher is to read the directions aloud to the students, instructing them to tell about the story by supplying past tenses in the sentences shown. If we are to take the directions literally, the students' responses are supposed to consist of single words: "telephoned," "was," and so on. What the author probably intended, however, was that students should produce the entire sentences, complete with past-tense verbs. This interpretation makes available several of the options that we have already examined: options 1 (whether to write in the books), 3 (choral or individual response), 4 (order of student response), and 5 (calling on students). It also leads to yet another option which is valuable in many kinds of activities:

OPTION 25: WHETHER TO HAVE STUDENTS DO FREE RECALL

a. Students respond only to the printed word or to cues from the teacher. Advantages: (i) This is the usual alternative, and so requires less attention. (ii) It saves time.
b. Students are invited to give, in any order, whatever facts they can remember from a drill, dialog, or other activity. Advantages: (i) Students are able to draw on verbal items which are still fresh from the other activity, but without depending on any external stimulus. (ii) Research on memory has shown that free recall, particularly if it requires a little effort, improves people's ability to get at the recalled items on later occasions. I suggest that whenever you use this alternative, you also choose alternative (d) of option 18 (repeating the

word/sentence correctly in whatever you say next) in dealing with any errors.

You can also extend the scope of this alternative. In its simplest, safest form, it would apply only to the material shown in activity A (see Figure 6.2), but if that goes easily, your students will probably respond well to the challenge of doing free recall from (*not* of!) the entire content (*not* language!) of scene 2.

Exercise 6.7

In activity B, we move from statements to questions. This part of the lesson draws on two dependable sources of nonverbal imagery: first the story and then the students' lives.

1. Which of options 1–25 (see list in appendix) are available here?
2. How would you conduct this part of the lesson?

COMMENTS

This is a neatly constructed drill which should have some success in its goal of helping students to use past-tense verb phrases. Although the activity has people directing words at one another, and although it is about a story that is rich in nonverbal imagery, it is still basically just a mechanical, noncommunicative drill. It is mechanical because there is really only one acceptable response to each question, and it is noncommunicative because everyone already has all of the information that is asked for (see exercise 2.1), and everyone *knows* that everyone else has this information.

Having students question and answer one another in this way is frequent in language classrooms. In the classes that I have taught or observed, however, the pace of this activity is plodding, and the level of animation is very low. Student A turns in her seat so as to half-look at student B, and pronounces the words of the question. Student B (if he is conscientious enough) turns in his seat before he pronounces the words of the answer. Both are aware of the teacher standing over them listening for mistakes.

If this seems to be happening in your class, you may want to apply option 19b (students talking with teacher): Student A asks the question of you, you relay the question (with any necessary corrections) to the student who is to answer, student B answers, and you then relay the answer back again to the questioner. You might even want to make sparing use of option 13b (making factual errors) here, just to keep people on their toes. Putting yourself into this triangle allows a bit of dramatization (option 12b) and the full range of alternatives for the use of your voice (option 14).

In a similar vein, you can let the students open their books and quiz you on your recall of details of scenes 1 and 2. Here again we have student initiative (option 8b) and the use of factual errors (option 13b). Students are practicing past questions, which is the main focus of this activity, and at the same time they are being exposed to various forms of answer (option 24b), complete with occasional appropriate flags.

The "Speakabout" section of Unit 2

Exercise 6.8

The sixth and last page of Unit 2 in the Student's Book is reproduced in Figure 6.3. There are two tape-recorded conversations that go with the lower half of the page.

Conversation 1
A Hello, Carol. How are you?
B Good, Jack. And you?
A Fine, thanks. Carol, do you have any plans for tonight?
B Well, I'm going to see a movie.
A Oh. What movie are you going to see?
B It's a French movie. My French teacher wants us to see it. She's going to ask us about it in class tomorrow. Do you want to come with me?
A Sure. Let's go.
B Okay. The movie starts at 8. Can you meet me at 7:30 in front of the library?
A Fine. See you at 7:30, then.
B See you soon, Jack.
A Goodbye, Carol.
B Bye.

Conversation 2
A Hey, Bob. Hi. *How are you doing?*
B John! Hey, *terrific!* And you?
A *Pretty good*, thanks. Hey, *are you* busy tonight?
B Well, I'm going to the game.
A What game?
B The *Jets!* They're *playing* Boston. Say, I have an extra ticket. *Can you* come?

SPEAKABOUT **2**

Making plans for the evening

You meet your friend on the street. You don't have any plans for the evening, but you feel like going out.

Listen to the sample conversations on the tape.

- Act out a similar conversation between you and your friend. Follow the conversation guide below. Some vocabulary cues are given, but you may choose words of your own.

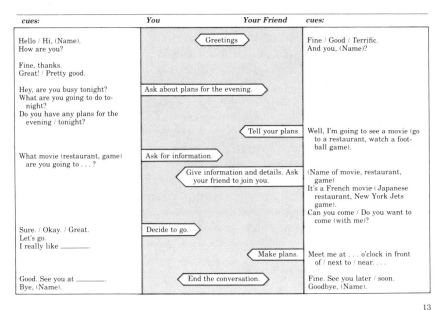

cues:	You	Your Friend	cues:
Hello / Hi, (Name). How are you?	Greetings		Fine / Good / Terrific. And you, (Name)?
Fine, thanks. Great! / Pretty good.			
Hey, are you busy tonight? What are you going to do tonight? Do you have any plans for the evening / tonight?	Ask about plans for the evening.		
		Tell your plans	Well, I'm going to see a movie (go to a restaurant, watch a football game).
What movie (restaurant, game) are you going to . . . ?	Ask for information.		
		Give information and details. Ask your friend to join you.	(Name of movie, restaurant, game) It's a French movie (Japanese restaurant, New York Jets game). Can you come / Do you want to come (with me)?
Sure. / Okay. / Great. Let's go. I really like _____.	Decide to go.		
		Make plans.	Meet me at . . . o'clock in front of / next to / near. . . .
Good. See you at _____. Bye, (Name).	End the conversation.		Fine. See you later / soon. Goodbye, (Name).

13

Figure 6.3. Page 13 from Unit 2 in *Transitions*, Student's Book, by Linda Ferreira. The material has been converted to black and white and reduced in size for reproduction here. (Reproduced with permission. © 1984 by Newbury House Publishers.)

Mostly about options

A Great. I really like football.
B I *can give you* a ride. Meet me at 6 o'clock at the corner of *86th Street and* Broadway.
A *See you* at 6 then.
B Fine.
A Bye, Bob. *See you* later.
B Bye, John.

The instructions for using the top half of page 13 read: "Students look at the photographs and read the opening statements which set the context. Refer to the photographs and ask: 'Where can you go?' (To a party. To a restaurant. To a football game.)" (Teacher's Manual, p. 13).

1. How is mental imagery handled in the top half of this page of the Student's Book?

COMMENTS

The Teacher's Manual of *Transitions* first states the goal of this page: "You meet your friend on the street ... and feel like going out." Students are to look at the pictures and talk about them. Then they work with the tape-recorded conversations. Finally, they "act out a similar conversation ..." This is certainly a more workable order than the order in which the pictures, tapescript, and instructions appear on the page of the Student's Book.

One question occurs to me about this page: Would it not be possible to select pictures which focus more clearly on the social aspects of the occasions that may enter into the plans of the people who are conversing? The picture of the movie marquee fully lighted but with no people in sight even seems a little eerie. The crepe paper streamer in the background of the second picture is the only evidence that this is a party, and not just a group of friends having their picture taken. The most conspicuous part of the third picture is the players, all on the same team, who are for the moment watching from the sidelines.

Exercise 6.9

The suggested procedure for using the pair of conversations is:
a. Play the tape of conversation 1, with students' books closed. Ask where Carol and Jack are, what they are going to see, and what time the movie starts.
b. Play the tape a second time, with students following the cues printed in the box at the bottom of the page. Help students with any unfamiliar words or expressions.

c. Play the tape of conversation 2, with students' books closed. Ask comprehension questions as in step (a).
d. Play the tape of conversation 2 a second time, with students again following the printed cues. Again help with any new words or expressions.
e. Get students talking about such questions as "Who's having a party?" "What movies are playing now?" "Where's a good place to meet near this school?"

1. How do the two conversations compare with dialogs J–1 (p. 20) and J–2 (p. 29) in Chapter 2?
2. What is their place in the overall economy of this page (Figure 6.3)?
3. What is the value of the three-column table at the bottom of the page?

COMMENTS

In this as in all units in *Transitions*, the pair of conversations in the listening section illustrate two different styles. Both are informal, but the first conversation consists mostly of complete sentences, and the rate of speech on the tape is moderate. The second conversation is "collapsed," with many sentence fragments, contractions, and idioms, and is spoken faster. The author is thus using both options 14b and 14c. She has also selected option 15b (the teacher assumes that students can already comprehend much that is in the lesson) and 17b (students hear the passage before they see it), which are surely right for almost any circumstances in which these conversations would be used.

Coming as they do in the middle of the page, the two conversations provide realizations of the context that was described at the top of the page, and at the same time they provide models on which students will be able to draw in the activities that follow them. The three-column table is, it seems to me, an excellent device. It lists the material in the conversations in a way which shows how, in spite of being different both in content and in style, the two are functionally identical. This sequence of functions is what students are to copy in the later activities; the words and phrases are only secondary to this purpose. The table throws the two model conversations into this perspective, and at the same time points away from them toward new and spontaneous creations of the students' own.

But if the two conversations are to serve as resources, the verbal items they contain must be readily available for the students to draw on. The steps listed in the Teacher's Manual may be sufficient for some classes. Other classes may need a bit more exposure. One way to provide it might be through intensive repetition after the tape or teacher, or even memorization. I suspect, however, that either of these would be quite time-consuming, and too "heavy" to hang onto an activity near the end of a long and varied unit. Another possibility would be comprehension questions or inference questions (option 23), but either of these would focus on content at a time when the emphasis of the lesson has quite rightly turned to function and to language use. Perhaps a better device would be to use paraphrase questions, which focus on function and carry forward the listing of cues in the table.

Exercise 6.10

The next-to-last activity in Unit 2 is referred to as pair work, in which:

Students follow the conversation guide [at the bottom of the page] to create similar conversations. Have students choose among the options for functional vocabulary [what we call *flags*], and expand with content vocabulary from their everyday experiences. Avoid having students write out lengthy dialogs. Encourage them to be spontaneous and work only from the cues in the text. [*Transitions*, Teacher's Manual, p. 13]

1. How would you organize this pair work?

COMMENTS

The wording of the instructions seems ambiguous. Are the students to create the new conversations in writing or orally? In either case, the teacher must decide what is to be done with these conversations once they have been created. If they are in written form, they present one choice:

OPTION 26: WHETHER STUDENTS SHOULD ATTEMPT TO CORRECT OR IMPROVE ONE ANOTHER'S WORK

a. All correction should be done by the teacher. Advantages: (i) This is the usual way. (ii) It takes no class time. (iii) Corrections can be more thorough and more authoritative.
b. One group looks at and edits the work of another, referring any doubtful items to the teacher. Advantages: (i) This makes use of the fact that people – and especially groups of people – are more accurate at recognition of correctness than they are at producing it. (ii) It gives students an extra area of involvement and responsibility. (iii) Any errors are dealt with while they are still fresh. (iv) It relieves the teacher of having to correct a stack of papers between classes.
    If the conversations are created in oral form, they present another pair of alternatives:

OPTION 27: WHETHER ENACTMENTS SHOULD TAKE PLACE IN FRONT OF THE WHOLE CLASS

a. Every group has a chance to act out its conversation in the presence of all. Advantages: (i) No groups need feel that their creation has died unseen. (ii) Any errors are exposed and made available for correction. (iii) This sort of conversation can sometimes be entertaining and instructive for all.
b. Each group performs before one other group, or two or three groups perform before the whole class. Advantages: (i) This saves time. (ii) There is less chance that the activity will become repetitious and start to drag.

FURTHER COMMENTS ON PAIR WORK

Whether the conversations are created orally or in writing, we still have a certain amount of choice regarding the degree of communicativeness. A conversation which simply puts new content into a prescribed functional context is communicative, but only in that the hearers do not know such details as whether the speakers are going to go to a movie or watch TV. There is no fixed information which is unevenly distributed at the beginning of the conversation and which must be exchanged in accordance with some series of purposes in order to complete some task. This activity, in addition to being low in communicativeness, is also almost "meaningless" (see exercise 2.5).

Two ways to increase the levels of meaning and communication in this particular activity might be the following: Create a series of starting points, for example:
- You're feeling great and have a lot of energy.
- You're tired and want to get to bed early.
- You have almost no money.
- You like/don't like watching sports.
Write each on a separate slip of paper and give *one* of them to *one* of the members of each group. The other member does not know what that information is.

Alternatively, you could assemble information about local movies, TV, athletic contests, and restaurants. Put each kind of information into a separate folder. According to the type of activity stated under "Tell Your Plans" (see table at bottom of Figure 6.3), the participants pick up and use one or another of these sets of information.

Exercise 6.11

The instructions in the Teacher's Manual for the last activity in the lesson are: "With a student, use the cues in the text to model a conversation."

1. What options does this activity imply?
2. How would you carry this activity out?

COMMENTS

This activity is potentially as low in meaningfulness and communicativeness as the pair work was (exercise 6.10). The teacher should therefore take full advantage of options 14 (use of teacher's voice), 12b (treating the material with a little pizzaz), and, if possible, 11b (attaching the meanings to individual students). This activity is also a natural setting for 18c–d (responding to errors of language).

If it follows the conversations created by the pairs of students, this activity may come across as an anticlimax. Conversation between teacher and student (option 19b) may also add to the resources out of which the pairs do their creating. For both these reasons, the teacher might consider placing this activity before the pair work instead of after it. On the other hand, if this activity follows pair work, it gives the teacher an opportunity to emphasize points at which the pairs have had trouble.

Summary

Of the books we have looked at so far, *Transitions* is the first that is written for students who are proficient enough to be able to talk back right at the beginning of the course. Most of the options that have been introduced in this chapter are accordingly concerned with the sources of what students say (whether they engage in free recall, whether they talk about their own inferences and interpretations, whether they react to one another's work, whether they stick to the language of printed dialogs). These options and this level of proficiency obviously open up exciting ranges of class activities. Certainly the teacher need not stick so meticulously within a well-known and sharply defined range of vocabulary and structure as at the lower levels. The temptation that comes with this enviable latitude is to try to do *anything* and *everything* that the teacher thinks would be fun to do with these people – to forget limitations just because the limitations are not so obvious. I suppose the answer is that the teacher should go ahead and enjoy the flexibility, but in a disciplined manner, and that he or she should still monitor the students' reactions just as consistently as with beginners.

In the literature

A helpful survey of ways of introducing new language is found in Chapter 6 of Harmer (1983). On the imaginative exploitation of students' ability to comprehend more than they can produce at this level, see Richards (1985), Grellet (1981), and Chapter 9 of Harmer (1983). Research reported by Buschke (1974) suggests that there may be important value in free-recall activities.

7 An advanced course

Functions of American English: Communication Activities for the Classroom, by Leo Jones and C. von Baeyer (Cambridge University Press, 1983) is for high-intermediate and advanced students, and is based on Jones's British text *Functions of English.* The published materials include a Student's Book, a Teacher's Manual, and an audiocassette.

The introduction to the Teacher's Manual explains that "the functional approach...involves isolating certain *language functions*, such as 'asking for information'...These functions are then learned by practicing them in a variety of everyday situations." "Situations," in turn, are described as involving various *roles* (friend, employee, customer, etc.), *settings* (on a plane, at a party, etc.), and *topics* (business, travel, sports, etc.).

The authors are careful to point out that the functional approach does not replace traditional teaching, and to suggest that grammar and vocabulary should be reviewed "in the usual way" when it appears that students have not yet mastered what they need. They also invite the teacher to exercise what I have called option 21 by adapting the printed materials and supplementing them as necessary.

In Chapters 4–6 we looked at sample lessons taken from three textbooks. If you have worked your way through those chapters, you are now familiar with the 27 options that we developed in them. There are still a few more options to be explored, but before we proceed it might be well to do a little reviewing and consolidating of what we have already covered.

The format of this chapter will therefore be a little different from the format of Chapters 4–6. Instead of looking at the materials one small part at a time as we did in those chapters, we will begin by looking at almost the entire set of general instructions to the teacher (Figure 7.2), taken from pp. 4–8 of the Teacher's Manual), and relating those instructions to everything in the earlier parts of this book. The individual exercises in Chapter 7 will require more time than most of the exercises in previous chapters, and some of the comments sections will be longer than heretofore.

Exercise 7.1

Figure 7.1 reproduces the first four (out of five) pages of Unit 7 in *Functions of American English*. Before you look at the the teacher's instructions in Figure 7.2, work through the following steps.

1. Spend 10 or 15 minutes reading carefully through the activities of Unit 7 and putting together your own ideas about how you would use them. Make a few written notes for yourself either in the margins of this book or on a separate sheet of paper. After you have done this, spend about the same amount of time leafing through the first six chapters of this book, looking for additional ideas that you might use with Unit 7.
2. Compare your ideas with those of the other members of your group. How did you differ among yourselves as to the kind and size of class that you imagined? How did you differ with respect to what you would do with the materials?
3. If your group is one part of a larger class or training seminar, report orally on any surprising or interesting differences that you noticed in step 2.

COMMENTS

Step 1 should of course be done outside of the class or group meeting. This exercise recognizes that you already know quite a bit (as in option 15c!) and requires you to take the initiative (option 8b) on a larger scale than before. It provides you an occasion to generate your own imagery of the class and of what you would do in the class, and in steps 2 and 3 (cf. alternatives (a) and (b) of option 19) it also provides a communicative and meaningful result for your having done so. The questions in step 1 are of the kind that require you to do your own thinking (option 23b). As you go through this exercise, you deal with the same task in a succession of ways (option 20b), and as you visualize yourself doing so your ideas will become more fully yours (option 11b). At the same time, your ideas will benefit from the comments of other members of your group (option 26b). This exercise will be a bit more time-consuming than earlier exercises, but the time will be well invested.

Exercise 7.2

Figure 7.2 (on pp. 122–6) reproduces pages 4–8 of the Teacher's Manual. These pages apply to all units in the book, not just to Unit 7.

7 *Offering to do something, asking for permission, giving reasons*

7.1   *Conversation*

John: Oh Anne, that was a wonderful dinner. That's the best meal I've had in a long time.
Anne: Oh thank you! Thank you very much.
John: Can I give you a hand with the dishes?
Anne: Uh-uh, don't bother. I'll do them myself later. Hey, would you like me to fix some coffee?
John: Uh, thanks a lot. I'd love some. Uh, would you mind if I smoke?
Anne: Why, not at all. Here, let me get you an ashtray.
John: Aw, thanks very much . . . Oh Anne, I, I didn't realize you were such a good cook.
Anne: [*laughs*] Actually, I've only just learned how, you know. It's because I've been taking these courses.
John: Why, I can't cook at all, can't even boil an egg.
Anne: No kidding. Well, you know, if you want to, you could take a couple of classes over at Sheridan College and learn how to do it too.
John: Aw, thanks a lot, but . . . I'm pretty busy these days.
Anne: [*laughs*]
John: Oh, I just remembered. Uh, I wonder if I could possibly use your phone.
Anne: Oo, I'm sorry, but it isn't working; it's out of order. Is it really important?

38

Figure 7.1. Pages 38–41 from Unit 7 in *Functions of American English*, Student's Book, by Leo Jones and C. von Baeyer (© 1983 by Cambridge University Press). The material has been reduced in size.

John: Well, you see, I have to call my foreman about tomorrow's work schedule. Uh, excuse me, would you, would you mind if I just went out for a few minutes? I'll give him a call from the phone booth on the corner.

Anne: Not at all. As long as you know your way back.

John: OK. I'll be right back.

7.2   *Presentation: offering to do something*

When something has to be done, you can ask someone else to do it, offer to do it yourself, or just do it without saying anything. If you want to be very polite when someone else is doing something, you can also offer to help. (This offer will often be refused.)

Here are some useful ways of offering to do something:

Let me get it for you.
Can I help you with that?
How about me getting it for you?
Would you like me to get it for you?
If you want, I could get it for you.
Any point in my getting it for you?

You might accept such offers with answers like:

Thanks a lot.
Oh, would you? Thanks.
That's nice of you, thanks.

Or refuse them by saying:

No, don't bother, I can do it myself.
No, it's all right. I can manage.
Thanks a lot, but I'm OK.

Decide with your teacher when you would use each of these expressions.

7.3   *Exercise*

Talk to your teacher and make some offers to help with his or her problems. Your teacher is bored, sick, lonely, thirsty, depressed, out of shape, hard up, hungry, and overworked. If you have time, do this with another student too.

7.4   *Communication activity*

Work in pairs. One person has some problems and the other person will offer to help. One of you should look at activity 91 while the other one looks at activity 63.

39

Figure 7.2 (cont.)

Mostly about options

7.5 *Presentation: asking for permission*

Sometimes you have to do more than just offer to do something – you may have to ask for permission to make sure you are allowed to do it. The expression to use depends on:

a) The type of task you want to do and the trouble you may have getting permission to do it.
b) Who you are and who you are talking to – the roles you are playing.

Here are some useful ways of asking for permission. The expressions get more and more polite as you go down the list:

I'm going to . . .
I thought I'd . . .
I'd like to . . .
OK if I . . . ?
Anybody mind if I . . . ?
Do you mind if I . . . ?
Is it all right if I . . . ?
Would it be OK if I . . . ?
Would you mind if I . . . ?
I wonder if I could possibly . . . ?
I hope you don't mind, but would it be possible for me to . . . ?

You usually give permission in just a short phrase, like:

OK.
Sure, go ahead.
Yes, I guess so.
All right.

And you refuse permission like this:

That's not a very good idea.
No, please don't.
I'd rather you didn't.
I'm sorry, but that's not possible.

Decide with your teacher when you might use each of these expressions. Give some examples of possible situations.

40

Figure 7.1 (cont.)

118

7.6　Exercise

Make a list of five things you would like to do but that you have to get your teacher's permission for. Ask for permission to do them – but watch out, your teacher may ask you why! Later your teacher will change roles and play the role of the head of the school, so then you may need to change the way you ask.

7.7　Presentation: giving reasons

When you ask people for permission, they are likely to ask you *Why?* Here are some useful ways of explaining your reasons:

Well, you see . . .
The reason is . . .
It's sort of complicated, but you see . . .
. . . and that's why I'd like to . . .
. . . and that's my reason for asking if I can . . .
Well, the thing is, . . .
It's because . . .

Discuss some ways to give reasons using these phrases (for example, if you wanted to borrow various things from your teacher).

7.8　Exercise

Make up conversations from the cues below, using expressions presented in 7.7. Follow this pattern:

A: Would it be all right if I left for a minute? I have to make a phone call.
B: I'd rather you didn't – the thing is, this is a very important part of the lesson.
A: I see. OK.

(Imagine that you are talking to an acquaintance, rather than to a close friend.)

leave room	have coffee break
smoke my pipe	borrow umbrella
borrow car	use phone
take day off	watch TV
open window	borrow book

7.9　Communication activity

Work in pairs. One person will ask for permission to do things while the other person plays different roles. One of you should look at activity 11 while the other one looks at activity 56.

41

Figure 7.1 (cont.)

Mostly about options

1. Spend 20 or 30 minutes reading carefully through these instructions, taking time to form mental images as you go.
2. Still working by yourself, make written notes of the points at which your results from exercise 7.1 are similar to the authors' suggestions, and of the points at which they differ.
3. Compare your results with those of the other members of your group.
4. If your group is part of a larger class or seminar, report on your findings in step 3.

COMMENTS

This way of approaching the authors' suggestions is analogous to option 18d: You have taken the initiative and now have a chance to compare your production with that of the experts. (One important difference, of course, is that in deciding how to use a given bit of material there are no "correct" or "incorrect" answers!)

Exercise 7.3

1. Examine the authors' suggestions again (Figure 7.2). Look especially at the ways in which they promote the development of mental imagery, both nonverbal and verbal. Then review the material in Chapters 1–3 of this book, keeping the authors' suggestions in mind.
2. As you did in the preceding two exercises, discuss your findings with other members of your group.
3. Report your results to the larger class or seminar.

COMMENTS

This Teacher's Manual provides rich opportunities for students to form and use imagery. Here are a few of them, in the order in which they appear in the guide.

a. *Content of conversation:* Although the cassette was obviously recorded in a studio, the recording is not the cleaned-up and careful style that language teachers instinctively use in order to make things easier for their students and to "set a good example" for them. That style is one which students recognize, and which carries with it the message, "This is textbook-talk for classroom study." That message limits the visual, emotional, and purposive items which the words arouse in students' minds. The more natural style chosen in *Functions...*, on the other hand, should make it easier for students to enter imaginatively into the interactions between the characters on the tape.

As we saw in our examination of both *Odyssey* and *Transitions*, the use of a set of continuing characters allows for accumulation of imagery from one unit to the next.

b. *Step 1 of the procedure for the conversation:* The teacher's talking about the conversation before it is played serves to begin the process of activation of relevant material from the students' existing verbal and nonverbal resources, yet without giving the story away. Students are left with questions for which the recording will provide some answers. In this way the mental work that the students must undertake as they listen is less than it would have been if the teacher had not described the characters and the general situation at all, but there is still plenty for them to do. This work receives a payoff immediately afterward as students engage in answering questions and discussing the relationship between the characters.

c. *Step 2 of the procedure for the conversation:* The suggestion to stop the tape before a speaker has finished (or before the next speaker speaks?) is a powerful one. It should certainly be workable with the advanced students for whom this book is intended, but it may also be useful for students on the level of *Odyssey* or *Transitions.* The authors do not specify whether this should be done during the very first playing, or whether it should be postponed until after the students have had a chance to hear the whole tape at least once. I would guess that either way is worth a try.

The authors comment that stopping the tape in the middle of the conversation "will help to train students to predict or anticipate what people are going to say." This is undoubtedly true, but it may be worth rephrasing in terms of mental imagery. Having to predict what someone is going to say is what in exercise 3.9 we called a task. As a matter of fact, this task can take either of two forms. The simpler of the two would be to predict only the content of what is about to be said, while the more difficult would be to try to predict both the content and the wording. (The latter would be an example of the cloze technique mentioned in Chapter 3.) In either form of this task, the student can no longer let the words flow in one ear and out the other. The student must now generate nonverbal imagery which fits what has already been heard, and this imagery must go well beyond the merely visual. It must include items which represent elements of setting, relationships, purposes, and emotional tone. This nonverbal imagery next becomes the basis for predicting, on the basis of schemata derived from the student's own earlier experiences, a set of nonverbal images about what the speaker on the tape is likely to want to communicate next. Having produced this nonverbal imagery, the student must next draw on his or her stock of verbal images (logogens) in the target language in order to express his or her predictions. Producing all of these verbal and nonverbal items, and then being rewarded both by meaningful and communicative com-

121

Conversation

Content

Each unit begins with a conversation that was recorded in everyday language, with all its hesitations and false starts. This is *not* a "dialogue" that the student should memorize. The conversation presents a performance in a typical situation of the functions focused on in the unit. In this way, students are introduced to some of the expressions that are used to carry out the functions, and they can see how the expressions are used by native speakers of English in a real conversation.

The situations involve two or three people at a time. The same six characters keep appearing in the situations, so the class will become familiar with them as real people:

Bob and Mary Graham – He works in an office, she at home.
John Spencer – He installs telephones but can't cook.
Anne Kennedy – She works in a trust company and likes John.
Sue Brown – She does photography and doesn't like violence on TV.
Ken Davis – He drives a big car and likes to smoke.

Procedure

A good way to use the conversations on tape is as follows:

1 Describe to the students the characters and the situation they are in, as given in the teacher's notes for each conversation. Play the entire conversation once or twice, and then ask general comprehension and summary questions. In later units, you may want to have the students guess the characters and situation after the first play-through, instead of telling them this information at the beginning. Discuss the relationship between the speakers.

2 Play the conversation, stopping it frequently before a speaker has finished, and ask: *What's he or she going to say next?* This will help to train students to *predict* or *anticipate* what people are going to say – an essential skill in understanding spoken English.

4

Figure 7.2. Pages 4–8 from *Functions of American English,* Teacher's Manual, by Leo Jones and C. von Baeyer (© 1983 by Cambridge University Press). The material has been reduced in size.

3 Play the conversation and ask the students to spot examples of the language functions being performed. Get them to mark these in their books. Discuss the effect of each example on the listener.

4 Discuss with the class any observations or problems arising from the conversation.

Giving more examples

The conversations can display only a few of the expressions that are presented in each unit, so you may have to give additional examples of your own to demonstrate the use of other expressions that you decide to present later on (see description of presentation sections that follows).

Variety

It is a good idea to use a variety of procedures with the conversations. Play a conversation section at the *end* of a unit occasionally. Concentrate more on step 2 (above) in one unit, more on step 3 in another. Sometimes use the alternative ideas suggested in the teacher's notes on each conversation.

Teacher's notes

The teacher's notes give the characters, situation, and topic(s) of each conversation, as well as alternative ideas for introducing each unit. The first three conversations are reproduced in the form of an annotated transcript, with the functions labeled and the expressions that are used to carry out the functions in italics.

Presentations

Content

The presentation sections include descriptions of the functions and various ways of carrying them out. Each unit usually has three presentation sections, each followed by various exercises and activities. One presentation section and its exercises might take about 45–60 minutes of class time to cover.

Procedure

Students should be asked to read these sections by themselves, preferably at home, before you cover them in class. A good way to handle the presentation sections is to have the students close their books and for you to use the tape and a blackboard. The tape presents expressions used to carry out the function under discussion in a lively way, and you can then provide further information and personal advice on how and when to use them correctly.

Alternatively, provided your class has thoroughly prepared itself for work on this section beforehand, you can call on the students to remember expressions, so that ideas will come from them – it is always better for students to make suggestions than for the teacher to "spoonfeed" them.

Whichever procedure you use, allow your students to introduce similar expressions from their own experience. Ask them to suggest examples of each expression in use. Make sure they can decide when each expression would be appropriate.

Changing the expressions

You are encouraged to change the lists of expressions that are provided in the presentation sections to suit your own or the local way of speaking. You should feel free to add, drop, or modify expressions. (If you are not sure about the appropriateness of an expression ask a native speaker

5

Figure 7.2 (cont.)

about it.) In any case, you may decide to concentrate your teaching on a selection of expressions that is not too easy or too hard for your class.

Choice
of
expressions

From the set of expressions that you cover in class – there should always be several for each function – your students should be free to choose a few as their own favorites. The focus of each lesson should be on *understanding* functions expressed in a *wide* variety of ways, but *expressing* functions in a *few* ways that the students feel most comfortable with. This element of choosing some expressions from a possible range is precisely what fluent speakers of a language do all the time – we know more expressions than we use, and we must always make a quick choice of one expression to use in any given situation. This is an essential ingredient of the functional approach.

Unpredict-
able
language

Some of the essential information is not given in the presentation section at all – often the most important thing is what students say *after* an introductory phrase. But since no once can predict what a student will actually say after *As I see it . . .* , for example, this information cannot be given in the book. Whatever students say, you must be prepared to provide some necessary vocabulary, to offer advice on usage, and to correct mistakes. True communication, which is the goal at this level of language learning, is often expressed through language that is unpredictable. Although dealing with this sort of unpredictable language may seem very demanding, it is certainly also extremely rewarding, and it is an essential part of training students to actually communicate their ideas.

Pronuncia-
tion and
simple drills

It may be necessary for you to do some controlled pronunciation practice – the tape will be useful for this. Students have to feel comfortable pronouncing an expression, especially if it's a long one, before they can start to use it. Pay particular attention to the tone of voice, for example, the polite and impolite way of saying *Would you open the window, please?* Apart from repetition of the new expressions in short sentences, your class may also benefit from some simple drills of the recommended expressions before moving on to the other exercises. In these simple drills, students need not produce complete, accurate communications but should use the recommended expressions in brief exchanges. Ideas for several such drills will be found in the presentation sections in the teacher's notes.

Teacher's
notes

Additional expressions that you may want to teach are given. There are also notes on points to watch out for and suggestions for some simple drills of the expressions being taught.

Exercises

There are three different kinds of exercise sections for practicing the material taught in the presentation sections. An exercise can take anywhere from 10 to 25 minutes to do.

Teacher-
controlled
exercises

The first exercise after each presentation is usually "teacher controlled," so that you have a chance to advise and correct your class before the freer exercise sections. Try to concentrate on helping the students to express themselves. Encourage them not to play safe but to experiment. Help them

6

Figure 7.2 (cont.)

to concentrate on using the recommended expressions. Encourage them to use some "new" expressions rather than just the "easy" expressions they know already. You may need to interrupt frequently during this first exercise section.

Freer exercises

The later exercise sections are much freer. They are designed to build confidence and fluency. Many of these sections require students to work together in pairs or small groups. It is important to set the scene very carefully in many of these exercises so that the students know exactly what they have to do and can get involved in the situation. Such scene-setting comes to life more if you do it in your own personal way, rather than relying on the printed words in the book.

Consolidation exercises

Finally, many units have a consolidation exercise at the end that practices expressions from all the presentations in the unit.

Procedures:

Monitoring students' performance

In the freer exercises, it is important not to interrupt students in the middle of a sentence or conversation just because a mistake has been made. This does not mean that you can sit back and relax – you should go around the room *monitoring* the conversations. This involves making notes of some good, and some not-so-good, ways of expressing oneself that you hear (these will be used later). Help students who are stuck, but try not to give too much help – otherwise the students will come to rely on you constantly. And don't correct every mistake – otherwise the students may become too mistake-conscious and tongue-tied. You will find the students correcting each other as they get used to such exercises, and this can be very effective if it is not overdone. Make sure you pause for questions after each exercise; this lets the students air their difficulties and gives you a chance to discuss what you heard as you went around the room.

Repeating exercises

You may find the students had so much trouble with a particular exercise that you want to do it all over again, perhaps in different groups. This kind of "replay" can increase confidence a lot and provide a tangible feeling of sudden progress that is often lacking at this level of language learning and that students often find reassuring.

The extra student

One minor problem in pair work is that in a class with an odd number of students, one person is left over after the rest of the class has paired off. This is easily solved by having the extra student share the work of one member of a pair. Suggestions for working with an extra student are given where necessary in the teacher's notes.

Changing partners

Do not allow students to talk to the same partner every time. Rearrange seating regularly or make sure that students change partners frequently. This will make conversations less predictable, and so more realistic. It will also make the exercises more interesting and lively – students can easily get bored with a regular partner.

Recording and performing

Once in a while, if possible, record a group in action (using audio or even video) and play back the recording for analysis by the rest of the class. From time to time ask a group to "perform" in front of the class after they have "rehearsed" their conversation.

7

Figure 7.2 (cont.)

Mostly about options

<table>
<tr><td>

Benefits of group work

</td><td>

The rationale behind pair or group work may need to be explained to students who feel that they should be corrected constantly by the teacher or that the teacher should control the whole lesson. Reasons for using pair and group work in this course include the following:

The amount of student talking time is greatly increased, and the more students talk, the more fluent they become.

Students feel less inhibited when talking privately to another student than when talking in front of the whole class. When they are less inhibited, they experiment more and discover how much they can actually communicate using the English they know already.

Playing roles in the exercises prepares students in a non-threatening way for the roles they may need to play in real-life situations in English.

</td></tr>
<tr><td>

Teacher's notes

</td><td>

Additional ideas for teacher-controlled exercises are given, as well as additional ideas for freer exercises.

</td></tr>
</table>

Communication activities

<table>
<tr><td>

Content

</td><td>

The freest, most open-ended exercises of all are the communication activities. These involve two or more sides communicating with each other in discussions, role plays, problem-solving activities, and so on.

</td></tr>
<tr><td>

Format

</td><td>

The communication activity sections in the individual units give instructions on (a) how to divide up the class, (b) the subject of the activity, and (c) with what activity number to begin in the *Communication activities* section at the back of the book. One activity at the back of the book often leads to another, until the students are instructed to reassemble as a class, discuss, and proceed in the unit they were studying. (A bookmark may come in handy for students to keep their places in the unit proper.)

</td></tr>
<tr><td>

Information gap

</td><td>

The actual activities are printed with the instructions for each group or individual student on different pages, so that the participants will not see each other's instructions. Don't allow students to prepare ahead of time or to "cheat" by looking at each other's instructions – the whole point of the communication activities is to *reveal* information to some students and *withhold* it from others who must try and get it. This creates the "information gap" or "uncertainty" mentioned at the beginning as one of the essential ingredients of genuine communication.

</td></tr>
<tr><td>

Procedure

</td><td>

In the communication activities, you have to trust the book to control the conversation; only step in when things are going too slowly or too fast. Try not to interrupt the flow of conversations in any way, but monitor the conversations and give help where it is needed. You may have to stop the activity at some point to make time for the very important discussion period. The students then report on what they did, and you and the class discuss their performance – not as actors but as speakers of English. The remarks made above on the procedures for freer exercises apply equally well to handling communication activities, particularly the remarks on monitoring the conversations, repeating activities, changing partners, and recording.

</td></tr>
</table>

8

Figure 7.2 (cont.)

parison of these images with the images reported by others as well as
by comparison with the tape, strengthens the nexuses among the items
that have been used and makes them more readily available for the
future.

The preceding paragraph is really nothing but a detailed translation
of the authors' suggestion into the terminology of mental imagery that
was developed in the first three chapters of this book. But if it is only
a translation, why not just leave it in everyday language? One answer
is that the translation is more detailed than the original. A more important answer, though, will lie in the extent to which the new phra-
seology reminds us of what has been learned about the content and the
formation of imagery, and about the ways in which images interact with
one another.

d. *Step 3 of the procedure for the conversation:* This suggestion calls
for students to begin with the verbal labels – supplied by book or teacher
– for various functions, and then to generate from this verbal material
some nonverbal items of purpose, to do the same with the words of the
conversation, and to compare the two sets of purposive items and find
where they match. All of this sounds rather abstract, but a very similar
technique worked quite well in a program with which I have firsthand
familiarity.

e. *Procedure for use with the "Presentations":* The alternative procedure given here is particularly promising from the point of view of
imagery. When the students suggest expressions – exponents or flags –
that they have met in their earlier experiences with the language, they
are engaging in a kind of "delayed free recall." The advantages of this
activity were discussed in connection with option 25 (whether to have
students do free recall).

Don't overlook the last sentence in this section of the Teacher's Manual either: "Make sure they can decide when each expression would be
appropriate." "Being exposed to" a series of alternative expressions is
relatively ineffective, and practicing such a list of expressions is only a
little more useful. Either of these activities *may* generate a bit of appropriate nonverbal imagery to go with the words. But a student who is
trying to *decide* when to use which expression *must* generate items having
to do with purpose, social status, and the like, in addition to items that
represent the basic meaning of sentences.

f. *Authors' comments on "Choice of Expressions":* Here the authors
suggest that the teacher allow students to settle on a few favorite ways
of handling each function, instead of asking them to use equally all of
the alternative expressions that they meet in the book and in class discussion. At the top of the following page, the authors tell the teacher
to "encourage students to use some 'new' expressions rather than just
the 'easy' expressions they know already." Are the authors contradicting

themselves here? I don't think so. I think they are validly presenting a very normal tension which exists in any healthy learning enterprise. What is at stake here is imagery on a level that we have barely mentioned up to this point: the student's picture of what kind of group this class is, and particularly of his or her relationship to the teacher. Is this a group in which an inappropriate usage can bring embarrassment or humiliation? Or does it consist of people who in a vigorous but relaxed way are pursuing a common goal? Is the teacher someone who only evaluates and corrects, or someone who understands and helps? (The approach which throws most light on this side of the learning experience is Counseling-Learning.)

g. *Authors' comments on "Unpredictable Language":* Expressions like "As I see it, . . . " or "If you don't mind . . . " are examples of flags. With regard to nonverbal imagery, flags represent items which have to do with the relationship that one utterance has to other utterances (or to wordless actions) within the purposes of the speaker. With regard to verbal imagery, the goal is to help the student to form a single, tightly knit and readily available logogen for the flag, no matter how many words the flag may contain. That is one of the purposes of the work with pronunciation and simple drills that the authors recommend in the next paragraph of the Teacher's Manual.

h. *Authors' comments on "monitoring students' performance":* The authors suggest that the teacher not interrupt students while they are in the midst of a practice exercise or communicative activity. They warn that interruptions may "make the students tongue-tied." That is true, but from the point of view that we are developing here there is a second reason not to interrupt: Switching the focus to the mechanics of the verbal side of what a student is doing at the moment will shatter the nonverbal imagery, or at least blur it. There is a time for focusing on the verbal, of course, and that is exactly what the authors are providing for when they recommend a few minutes for questions and discussion at the end of each exercise.

i. *The "Information Gap":* Much is made these days of the value of having an information gap between what one student knows and what another knows. To take a simple example, one student knows how many brothers and sisters Anne Kennedy has, another knows where she was educated, another knows how much money she makes, and at the end of the exercise all students have all the facts. Another example, a communication activity taken from the Student's Book for Unit 7, is designed for practice of asking and giving permission. Student A plays the role of an employee. He or she is instructed to "ask your boss to let you change your vacation from next week to the week after." Student B, the boss, receives the instruction "You are the boss. Your partner, who works for you, will make a request. He or she is one of your most dependable employees." In this exercise both students know who is the boss and who is the employee and that a request will be made. Only Student A knows what the request is to be, while only Student B knows how this particular employee and his or her request are likely to be regarded by the boss. The existence of such a gap was the criterion given earlier for determining whether or not to call a given activity communicative, and the authors of *Functions of American English* make excellent use of it.

But the information gap – the uneven distribution of facts among the people in the classroom – is only one special case of a broader principle, which we can call "unfinished business." With or without an information gap that either of them cares about, the participants in a conversation may be trying to make plans, or to persuade one another of the conclusions to be reached from the facts at hand, or to amuse each other, or to commiserate, or even to put each other down. In everyday use of language, two or more types of unfinished business are commonly at work at the same time. And it is unfinished business of *any* kind, not just the sharing of facts, that calls for and thus stimulates fuller nonverbal imagery. In this sense there is value in such activities as discussing a film that all have just seen, or doing role plays which are not constrained by a full set of external facts. Even something so prosaic as talking about the locations of objects in the classroom can have this effect if there is some unfinished business around. On the other hand, an information gap with no other kind of unfinished business can quickly become perfunctory; who really cares how many siblings one's classmates have, or where the teacher has just hidden the ruler?

Exercise 7.4

1. Which of the comments on imagery in the authors' suggestions (exercise 7.3) did you anticipate in the three steps of that exercise? Which ones did you not anticipate? Which ones, if any, seem particularly valuable? Which ones, if any, seem less so?
2. Spend a short time comparing your reactions in step 1 with the reactions of other members of your group.

Exercise 7.5

1. Now examine the authors' suggestions once more. This time, look at them in terms of the 27 options that were developed in Chapters 4–6 and are summarized in the appendix. Make marginal notes for use in steps 2 and 3.

2. As in the earlier exercises in this chapter, discuss your findings with other members of your group.
3. Report your results to the larger class or seminar.

COMMENTS

The decision to use normal speech in the recording is an instance of option 14c. Not requiring the students to memorize the conversation is certainly an example of not requiring them to reproduce it (option 22b), but it raises an issue which divides the famous Audiolingual Method from much that went before it and has come after it. This is in fact worth listing as an added option:

OPTION 28: WHETHER STUDENTS SHOULD MEMORIZE DIALOGS OR OTHER MATERIAL

a. Memorization was standard audiolingual practice. The advantage is that students can draw on what they have memorized in order to build up a stock of verbal images – logogens – which can help them to succeed in many other types of activity, all the way from mechanical drills to genuinely interesting free communication. I hit on this expedient myself in 1942, some years before the terms *Oral Approach* or *audiolingual* were ever coined. But I'm one of those for whom memorization is easy and even sometimes unintended.

b. Students should not be required to memorize texts. Memorization can be very time-consuming for many people, and some people have strong emotional reactions against it. This option is pretty much a dead one in most circles these days, but it should not be omitted from our list.

In the procedure for step 1 (Figure 7.2) of work with the conversation, the authors are clearly expecting the teacher to take the initiative (option 8a), to conduct the activity in a straightforward rather than a dramatic way (option 12a), and to have the students hear the conversation before they see it (option 17b). In the first part of step 1, the authors refer to "comprehension and summary questions" (option 23a, where answers come from the text), but the discussion which they recommend at the end of the paragraph represents the other alternative (option 23b, where answers require students to draw on the nonverbal imagery derived from the text). The teacher may of course choose to go from easier to harder questions or the reverse (option 10), and replies may be either in complete sentences or in colloquially authentic sentence fragments (option 24). (Which alternatives from options 10 and 24 do you think you would choose if you were working with these materials?)

Asking students to spot examples of functions and then to mark the examples in their books is an obvious instance of option 1a, but because what is being written into the book does not consist of answers to practice activities, the option does not have the disadvantages that it sometimes has.

The suggestion to change the relative emphasis given to successive steps in the basic procedure, or even to change their order occasionally, is an apt one. Perhaps it deserves to be listed as a separate super option!

In working with the "presentations" in each lesson, the alternative of having students remember examples of functions, instead of spoonfeeding them, of course implies options 8b (student initiative) and 25b (free recall). The invitation to add, drop, or modify the expressions in the book is a small-scale example of super option 21b. The invitation to add drills on pronunciation or structure is a larger-scale example of the same option.

Redoing activities with different groupings or with different partners allows students to get additional practice with logogens which are still fresh in their minds, and which are therefore relatively "inexpensive" in terms of time and effort. This serves to tie these words in with additional items of fact, purpose, emotion, and all the rest, and so is a means of implementing option 20b (multiple use of materials). The switch suggested by the authors, from being an actor *in* a role play or other communicative activity to standing back and speaking *about* what was done during that activity, has the same effect. In addition, it allows students to shift focus from content (nonverbal meanings) to form (getting the verbal side right), and so to work with words for which the meanings are still comparatively fresh, full, and clear in their minds. This makes a lot more sense than the reverse: first assembling the words and grammatical structures, and then casting about for some meaningful and communicative ways to use them!

Exercise 7.6

1. Which of the options mentioned in the preceding exercise did you anticipate as you were doing that exercise? Which ones did you not anticipate? Which ones, if any, seem particularly valuable? Which ones, if any, seem less so?
2. Spend a short time comparing your reactions in step 1 with the reactions of other members of your group.

Exercise 7.7

The Teacher's Manual contains a number of phrases which include the word *function*:

People can *learn* functions.
Students should *practice* functions.
This unit *focuses on* certain functions.
Have students spot *examples of* these functions.
Certain functions are *being performed* in this conversation.
Expressions are used in order to *carry out* this function.
This function can be *expressed* in a variety of ways.

1. The functional approach which *Functions of American English* represents is often contrasted with the structural approach. Working with a group of other people if possible, try replacing the word *function* with the phrase *point of grammar* in each of these sentences. Which substitutions make sense, and which do not?
2. Try to settle on a word or short phrase which could be used as a synonym for *function* in all of these examples. (*Purpose? Thing to be done?* Something else?)

COMMENTS

Although I recognize the great value of the recent emphasis on communicative competence and on functions, I have always been a bit uneasy about some of the ways in which these two terms – and particularly the latter – get used. Finocchiaro and Brumfit (1983: 13) define *functions* as "communicative purposes" or "what people want to accomplish through speech acts," and this definition is consistent with what most other authorities on the functional approach seem to be saying. So we can ask students to "spot examples of " purposes, or to "focus on" certain purposes, or to "express" purposes. But it is not clear what it means to ask students to "learn" or to "practice" purposes. Yet we run into the expressions "learn functions" and "practice functions" in many writings on the functional approach. In spite of the fact that the functional approach has often been viewed as parallel to (or perpendicular to!) the structural approach, students cannot really learn or practice functions (which are nonverbal items of purpose) in the same sense in which they can learn or practice points of grammar (which are restrictions on and relationships among verbal items).

A related difficulty I find in much talk about functions is that people often seem to say, "The function of this sentence is to make a request," or "The function of that sentence is to accept an offer." The problem lies in saying "*the* function," because any one sentence is likely to be serving more than one purpose at the same time. Of course, any sentence except the very shortest also exemplifies more than one grammatical structure at the same time. But the grammatical structures are placed end-to-end, or they are embedded in one another according to a set of rules that determine which word or prefix or suffix comes after which other word or prefix or suffix. The verbal *form* of language is thus produced in a single dimension – the dimension of time.

The nonverbal *purposes* of a given sentence may make up some sort of loose hierarchy, too. But the members of such a hierarchy exist in many dimensions simultaneously, and so they do not tie in clearly with the succession of words and prefixes and suffixes that come from the mouth of a speaker or from the pen of a writer. Thus, for example, we can say quite correctly that *a* function of Anne's "Don't bother. I'll do them myself." is "to decline an offer." But what was her purpose in declining the offer? Perhaps it was to keep John from seeing the messy kitchen, or perhaps to make the evening as pleasant for John as possible, or to appear as a vigorous, efficient, self-reliant person, or quite possibly some combination of these. If we come back and ask again, "But *why* did she want to make the evening pleasant, or come across as vigorous and self-reliant?" the answer might be "to make a good impression on John." The further "why?" for that might be answered, "to promote the development of their friendship," and so on. At each step in this series of questions other responses are possible: There are other reasons for trying to come across as self-reliant than to make a good impression, and there are other reasons for trying to make a good impression than to promote friendship. But whatever the series of purposes may be, all of them exist at once. Any or all of them may influence the linguistic form of a sentence, but not in the neatly mappable way in which grammatical structures do so. You can apply this principle directly in the classroom, too, asking a series of "Why? Yes, and why? Yes, but why?" questions at step 1 or 3 of the authors' procedure for use with the conversation. Such a series of questions would also fit naturally into the little technique that we examined in exercise 2.3. A linguistically less demanding activity would be to ask students to select from a list of possible motivations those that seem to apply to various parts of the conversation.

There is a third characteristic of functions which I think deserves more attention than it has usually received: the fact that they often occur in sequential clusters. A simple example is found in Unit 2 of *Functions . . .*, where there are several instances of "to accept an offer" or "to decline an offer." But, referring again to the Finocchiaro-Brumfit definition of *functions* as communicative purposes or what people want to accomplish through speech acts, there are commonly several things that people want to "accomplish" in accepting or declining an offer. One is to state explicitly whether the offer is being accepted or declined. Another is to express thanks. A third is to make some comment about the person who made the offer. A fourth is to give information about the reason for accepting or declining. So in response to "May I help you with that bag?" the reply might be:

Why, yes, thank you!

You're very kind!

It *is* pretty heavy! (*accompanied by nonverbal action of relinquishing the handle of the bag*)

or any one of these or just about any combination of two or more of them, one following after another. Similarly, the offer frequently involves the accomplishing of such smaller functions as "to get attention," "to indicate the reason for an offer," and "to make the offer easier to accept," as well as the offer itself:

Here, Bill!

That bag's too heavy for you!

Let me take it!

I'm a lot bigger than you are.

This principle also is useful as well as interesting. The authors of *Functions* . . . suggest that the teacher invite the students to come up with other *expressions* which could perform the same functions as those in the "Conversation" and "Presentation" sections of the textbook. As they point out, this kind of practice has considerable value, because the discussion itself produces communicative use of the language in the performance of a genuine task. The same would be true for the task of picking out *subfunctions* of the kinds I listed earlier. This task also forces students to pull together a large amount of nonverbal imagery, which further enhances the value of their practice with the linguistic forms found in the conversation. At the same time it requires a much sharper look at the rules of discourse, and may even lead the students to identify a few interesting cross-cultural differences.

Exercise 7.8

Although their textbook is clearly committed to the functional approach, the authors say that grammar must still be learned, and that when students' performance in functionally oriented activities shows that they have not mastered a bit of grammar, the grammar should still be "reviewed in the usual way." Because the conversations in *Functions* . . . are quite idiomatic, they contain numerous examples of points which lie just a little outside what in exercise 2.7 we called Intuitively Safe Grammar.

1. From the conversation between Anne and John (Figure 7.1), select a point of grammar which high-intermediate students may not yet have

mastered. Compare your selections with those made by other members of your group.
2. Write a simple drill on this point. (You may wish to refer to Chapter 3 of this book or to other books on methods for some ideas about the construction of drills.)
3. Get the other members of your group to comment on your drill.

COMMENTS

If the point selected for practice happens to be the use of *even* as in "I can't even boil an egg," one could write some such drill as:

	I can't even boil an egg.
drive a car	I can't even drive a car.
carry a tune	I can't even carry a tune.

At the high-intermediate or advanced level, however, this simple sort of cue-word-followed-by-response drill is less appropriate than it might have been at the lower levels of linguistic proficiency. There are really two problems in this way of using *even*. One is its place in the sentence: Some learners are likely to say "I even can't..." The second has to do with its meaning, which implies a kind of quantitative comparison of two ideas. The preceding drill requires students to focus only on the first of these problems. A drill which involves both form and meaning is:

Combine the sentences in each pair into a single sentence using *even*:
1. I can't boil an egg.
   I can't cook.
       I can't cook; I can't even boil an egg.
2. I can't speak French.
   I can't read French.
3. He has won a prize for singing.
   He can sing quite well.

Students must understand the sentences in order to be able to decide which member of each pair should have *even* in it.

After a bit of practice of this kind, students and teacher can make up similar statements about themselves and one another.

Exercise 7.9

In exercise 7.7, we said that functions cannot be drilled in the same sense that grammatical structures can be. Nevertheless, there may be a time for a little compact and tightly focused practice with expressions that are commonly used for accomplishing some of the purposes that people have when they talk.

135

Mostly about options

1. Try your hand at designing such a function drill for the functions that are featured in Unit 7 (Figure 7.1).
2. Compare your drill with the ones produced by other members of your group.

COMMENTS

COMMENTS

One possible kind of function drill is:

The teacher will ask you for permission to do something. Reply with one of the following expressions:
That's not a very good idea.
No, please don't.
I'd rather you didn't.
[etc.]

Here, very much as in the first drill in the comments on exercise 7.8, the student can succeed by concentrating entirely on the form of the expressions. This is probably not challenging enough for high-intermediate or advanced learners, however. Such a drill can be improved by having the teacher assume different roles – friend, boss, stranger on a bus, and so on – and having students modify their replies accordingly. This is in line with one of the suggestions made by the authors of *Functions...*

The following function drill is compact, but it still requires students to pay attention to meaning as well as to form. It takes advantage of the fact that Unit 7 is about two similar but still different pairs of functions: making and responding to a request, and asking and giving/ withholding permission.

The teacher will say something to you. If it is an offer, reply with an expression from list A. If it is a request, reply with an expression from list B.

Students are provided with the two lists either on the board or on paper. The lists should contain some items that have been suggested by the students themselves in earlier discussion.

Summary

In the past few years, there has been a surge of interest in the functional side of language. This movement within the profession is understandable and commendable, both as a relief from the language teacher's traditional preoccupation with either the form of language or its literature, and in its own right as an attempt to make use of newly gained knowledge. As often happens, however, enthusiasm for concepts has not always been matched by precision in talking about them. I have mentioned some of my own concerns in this respect and have tried to deal with them. This book is not, however, the place for theoretical discussion. These issues continue to receive further attention in professional periodicals and books.

In the literature

Berns's (1984: 7) discussion of function in the tradition of Firth and Halliday is clear and helpful. Chapter 3 of McArthur (1983) summarizes the notional-functional and related approaches. (See especially section 3.7.) An entire book devoted to this approach is Finocchiaro and Brumfit (1983). The slightly skeptical view of a thoroughly experienced practitioner is found in Swan (1985).

A number of the games in Wright, Betteridge, and Buckby (1984) tap into personal agenda which are not specific to language learning but which are deep and are found in most people. Two examples are the games on page 41 which require students to estimate the relative lengths of lines – a basic skill which in other contexts has primal value for the survival of individuals and species!

8 Other kinds of teaching material

In Chapters 4–7 we looked at four different sets of materials. All four consist entirely or principally of books, and all four are good representatives of directions in which the language teaching profession has been moving since approximately the mid-1970s. Among them they cover the full range of student proficiency, from pre-beginner to advanced. We explored how concepts of verbal and nonverbal imagery might cast light on the use of these materials, and we discovered that many of the same options are available in most or all of them.

In this closing chapter we will look first at a lesson taken from an older textbook with a rather traditional format, and then at three kinds of material which do not consist of books at all. As before, our goal will be to apply imagist thinking to all of them and to explore options.

An older textbook

Although the materials that we have examined in the earlier parts of this book have differed greatly in format, type of syllabus, and teaching techniques as well as in the proficiency levels for which they were intended, they have in common the fact that all were published in the first half of the 1980s. Not everyone who reads this book, however, will be using textbooks which come from this particular historical period. If the options that we have explored, and the concepts of item, network, image and the rest are of permanent interest to language teachers, then they should be applicable also to quite different courses taken from other traditions.

It is for this reason that I have included in this last chapter a section on a textbook published in 1967. The title of the text and the authors' names will not be mentioned, since the aim of this section is not to criticize the work; indeed, I'm sure that neither of the authors would write this kind of course today. I must also confess that this textbook is not very different from one or two that I worked on for other languages in the 1960s.

Each of the lessons in this book contains most but not necessarily all of the following types of activity: repetition drills, substitution drills, transformation drills, appropriate-response drills, question-and-answer drills, and directed-discourse drills.

This is a textbook that was intended for both absolute and false beginners at the elementary and intermediate levels of study. The authors' stated goal was to provide a textbook for adults covering, with a limited vocabulary of high-frequency words, those *"features of English phonology and syntax which students should be able to comprehend and manipulate before* proceeding beyond the intermediate level." They kept vocabulary to a minimum in order to permit the student to *"concentrate on mastering basic sentence patterns."* The authors believe that "students who master all of the material should have a firm *foundation on which to build when they go on to the advanced levels"* (emphasis added in all quotations).

Exercise 8.1

1. Examine the quotations in the previous paragraph from the point of view of mental imagery.
2. Discuss your comments with other teachers. Have any of you ever used materials comparable to this textbook? If so, does that experience seem to affect your reactions to the quotations?

COMMENTS

We have here an unusually succinct and clear statement of the basic assumptions of the Audiolingual Method: that the patterns of the language should be learned first, that they should be learned by practice, that students need only a minimal awareness of the meanings of the forms that they are practicing, and that once these forms and these patterns had been established firmly in this way, meaningful use (apparently what these authors have in mind when they speak of the "advanced level") can be accommodated by combining the patterns and adding vocabulary.

This kind of teaching focused first and for a long time almost entirely on the verbal resources – the logogens – that would enable students to put sentences together correctly within a limited vocabulary. Nonverbal imagery was slighted. The method frequently led to problems with "transfer": students who could handle a grammatical point perfectly in class but who seemed to forget all they knew as soon as they walked out the door of the classroom. From the imagist point of view of this book, such problems are hardly surprising. Experience outside the classroom – the experience which calls for the use of language – includes nonverbal items of purpose and emotion (as well as real people and objects) to which no nexuses had been formed inside the classroom. Access to the needed verbal items was therefore slow and uncertain. At least this may be one partial explanation!

Lesson 5 of this older textbook begins with a nine-line dialog between a teacher and Marcos Perez, a student:

Are you from Bolivia?
Yes, I'm from La Paz.
That's an interesting city.
Yes, it is.
Is your family in La Paz now?
My parents are. But my brother's in Seattle.
Is he a student?
No, he's a businessman.

Exercise 8.2

One possible goal of work with a dialog is complete memorization (option 28a). To achieve that goal requires large investments of time and energy. The process of investment can be long and tiresome. Frequent switching of alternatives can lighten the burden considerably. In fact, it was in my days as an audiolingual teacher that I first discovered the value of some of the simpler options.

1. List as many workable combinations as you can from the alternatives in options 2 (timing of student responses), 3 (choral vs. individual response), 4 (order of student response), 5 (calling on students), 6 (moving through the materials), and 18 (responding to errors of language).
2. Exchange your list with someone else. Challenge any combinations that you don't think are actually workable.
3. Make a composite list based on consensus from step 2.

COMMENTS

The real purpose of memorization was never just that students should recite a long stretch of prose for its own sake, but only that students should have the various components of that prose available for use in the future. Another way of increasing the availability of such components is to read the fixed dialog to students a number of times, changing a word here and a word there. Students are required only to indicate where they hear changes, and to say what the original word or phrase was. This is one more application of option 13b, in which the teacher makes errors of fact that do not violate the language.

The content of the dialog quoted from Lesson 5 lends itself to option 11b, using names and facts that apply to the students in the class instead of sticking with Marcos Perez and Bolivia. This should increase both the palatability and the memorability of the exercise.

Exercise 8.3

The next three activities in this lesson are "Questions About the Dialogue," "Sentences for Repetition," and "Substitution Drills":

Questions About the Dialogue
Is Marcos Perez from Bolivia?
Is he from La Paz?
Where is his brother now?
...

Are you from La Paz?
Are your parents from La Paz?
[etc.]

Sentences for Repetition:
I'm in Miami.
You're in Miami.
Marcos is in Miami.
...

Your family's in Bolivia.
His brother's in New York.
Their teacher's from Miami.
[etc.]

Substitution Drills:

Teacher	Student
It's my book.	
pen	It's my pen.
hat	It's my hat.
...	
They're my pencils	
shoes	They're my shoes.
watches	They're my pencils.
[etc.]	

1. On the basis of your own experience, what do you think would be the relative effectiveness of this sequence of activities in building verbal images (logogens)? In building nonverbal images?
2. If you were teaching in a program where this book was the required text, and if you knew your students were going to have to pass a test based on it, how could you exercise options from among 1–28 (see list in the appendix) in order to improve your students' ability with English?

COMMENTS

The problem posed by this exercise is a tough one, but it is no more difficult than problems faced every day by many teachers around the world. Although all of the sentences are grammatically correct, and although it is possible to imagine situations where they might be used, they are here produced with no reference to anything in the vicinity of the students. This is especially noticeable in sentences like "They're my watches." (How many people carry more than one watch?) These sentences are thus "meaningless," as we used that term in exercise 2.5, and being meaningless they are also necessarily noncommunicative. It would therefore seem wise to take these forms and attach them to whatever meanings are handy – in this case information about the students and their families. One possible stratagem for doing so is the following:

a. Make the verbal images available by having students (i) repeat the sentences of the drills with books closed and then with books open, and then (ii) do the drills briefly as recommended using alternatives from options 2 (timing of student responses), 3 (choral vs. individual response), 4 (order of student response), 5 (calling on students), 6 (moving through the materials), and 17 (hearing before reading). The availability of the verbal images will disappear almost immediately if the forms are not quickly given some sort of meaningful use.

b. Shifting out of the "teacher" style and into the role of an interested person (option 12b, dramatizing), point to various things that belong to the students and ask, "What's that?" (option 11b, personalizing). Or use the same options in asking questions similar to the ones in the "Questions About the Dialog."

c. Ask the students questions that they can answer by using sentences with the same form as those in the book, as if to verify whether or not they have remembered the information that pertains to the others.

This stratagem is admittedly only a beginning, and a not very brilliant beginning at that! Perhaps you will be able to come up with something more effective and maybe even a little exciting. But brilliant or not, it is at least better than trudging through the activities as they are given in the book. Step (a) points to one more option – an option we have had available with all of the materials we have looked at:

OPTION 29: WHETHER TARGET-LANGUAGE WORDS AND SENTENCES SHOULD BE TRANSLATED ORALLY INTO THE STUDENTS' NATIVE LANGUAGE(S)

a. The advantages of avoiding oral translation are well known: (i) With translation, the students have less reason to call up and work with their existing verbal and nonverbal resources, and (ii) the teacher is more likely to be careless about bringing in more material than the students can assimilate. (iii) The teacher will also be less likely to bother with supplying a full range of live nonverbal items to go with the words and sentences of the lesson. (iv) Time spent in translating or in hearing the teacher's translations is not available for practice in speaking and comprehension of the target language.

b. The only advantage I can think of for having the teacher or students translate orally is to make certain that the students have in their heads at least some appropriate nonverbal imagery to go with the words to which they are being exposed. With well-designed materials, it will be possible to do without translation entirely or to use very little of it. The nonverbal images that translation produces for most people are probably stale, flat lowest-common-denominator meanings which contain little in the way of immediate emotion, purpose, or even visual specificity. But without them most of the activities quoted from the textbook that we have been looking at would be little but unintelligible noise. So in the real world...

Rods

Rods are small rectangular pieces of wood or plastic. The cross section of each rod is one centimeter square. There are ten lengths, from one to ten centimeters. All rods of a given length have the same distinctive color. A set of rods includes at least six of each length.

Most people prefer to work with the wooden variety. Wooden rods are lighter in weight and more pleasant to the fingers, and make a livelier sound when dropped on a tabletop. Some people prefer the plastic ones, which have the advantage of being washable.

Rods are often called *cuisenaire rods*, after Georges Cuisenaire, the European educator who first used them. He apparently confined them to the teaching of mathematics, and to this day many people know them as *math rods*. Cuisenaire's work was observed by Caleb Gattegno, who incorporated rods into his Silent Way of teaching, first in mathematics and later in foreign languages. Practitioners of the Silent Way sometimes call them *Algebricks*. But rods by any name offer a better combination of effectiveness, flexibility, and economy than any other teaching aid I have seen.

The use of rods

Why use rods? Rods appeal to the senses. Therefore they *attract* and *hold* students' *attention*.

143

Rods are simple in shape and color. Therefore they *concentrate* students' attention.

Rods have no unnecessary markings or details of shape. Therefore they present an open field for the students' *imagination*. They are like concrete abstractions which we can put to an incredibly wide range of uses.

Almost anyone who is teaching anything can probably make good use of a set of rods. Language teachers in particular can employ them with students at all levels, from absolute beginners on up. Since each color has its own length and intensity, even colorblind people can learn with rods. At least one teacher who was totally blind used rods with her classes.

A simple game or a lively exercise with rods is an excellent warmup at the beginning of a class while stragglers are still arriving.

During a class session, rods let students see and handle some of the abstractions thay they may find hard to follow in an explanation that consists only of words.

Rods can also serve as a welcome visual channel for expressing concretely what two or more people are talking about. This is often a good way to end an hour.

For most purposes, rods should be used against a plain background. If there is anything else on the tabletop with them, it will intrude on the students' awareness and so detract from the rods' power to concentrate attention.

Don't hesitate to use rods in large classes. They have been used successfully in classes as large as 70. Perhaps because they are so easy to concentrate on, students can see them from far greater distances than either you or they would expect.

The longest-established uses of rods for teaching languages are in the Silent Way. The Silent Way is an approach to teaching anything to anyone, but its implications extend far beyond the classroom. I believe that study of the Silent Way provides a discipline which will make any teacher a better teacher no matter which methods she or he uses later on.

This chapter will tell you nothing about rods in the Silent Way, however. Gattegno's books are an infinitely better guide for that purpose. But just as the Silent Way does not depend on rods, so rods can be used outside the Silent Way. The pages that follow will explore only two of countless techniques. Because the emphasis of this book is on imagery and options rather than on techniques, I have thought it best to choose three of the simplest and most obvious techniques. Elsewhere I have described a few of the more sophisticated techniques with rods (Stevick 1980: ch. 5, 6, 11; Stevick 1982: 72, 80, 129, 131, 138). Readers may want to try their hands at applying these same concepts of imagery and options to those techniques.

Exercise 8.4

The following is one way of using rods.

Rod Technique 1: "Missing Link"

Goals: Linguistic: practicing names of colors as single words or in the context of simple sentences. Functional: engaging in the solicitation and giving of advice.

1. Using rods, build on the table three sides and part of the fourth side of a rectangle.
2. Ask students for the color(s) of the rod(s) needed to complete the rectangle.
3. Let the students reply spontaneously.
4. Try out suggestions as you hear them, until the figure has been completed correctly. Then begin a new figure.

1. What is the functional side of this activity?
2. What language would you use in conducting it?

COMMENTS

From a functional point of view, this activity in its simplest form consists of three turns: a request for help, the offering of a suggestion, and the trying out of the suggestion. The first and third of these turns offer a new choice:

OPTION 30: WHETHER TO PERFORM COMMUNICATIVE FUNCTIONS THROUGH WORDS OR THROUGH ACTIONS ONLY

a. The function is carried out through the use of language. Advantages: (i) This is what students and teacher are probably used to. (ii) Students get to hear language in the context of physical action. (iii) Students may be exposed to a wide range of exponents (exercise 7.3), from rather formal ("Which color rod will complete this rectangle?") to more colloquial ("Now, let's see. What do I need here?" or "Which color shall I try?" or the like). This latter choice is a special case of option 7, in which the teacher varies the linguistic form for a narrow range of meanings that students can anticipate.
b. The function is carried out without words. Advantages: (i) Students can concentrate more sharply on what they are saying. (ii) Students develop and demonstrate the nonverbal skill of estimating physical sizes. This personalizes the students' suggestions (option 11b) and can become the occasion for a little nonlinguistic competition. To that extent, the teacher's silence provides an opportunity for one kind

of drama (option 12b). (There are also plenty of ways to dramatize with alternative (a), as well!) In a nonverbal counterpart of option 9b-c (hiding words), you can vary the size and complexity of the figure. One possibility is to make a small rectangle with three complete sides, but with no fourth side. Another is to build part of the fourth side also, with a 2–10 cm gap.

Exercise 8.5

1. Which of options 1–30 (see list in appendix) are present in "Rod Technique 1"? Which alternatives from those options are implied?
2. How might you use other alternatives from these same options with this technique?

COMMENTS

As described previously, "Rod Technique 1" chooses the most common alternatives from two of the options in earlier chapters: Interaction is between teacher and students (option 19b), and the teacher takes the initiative (option 8a). Depending on the class, you may decide to change alternatives for either or both of these options. Several other options are clearly open: the order in which to call on students (option 4), how to indicate which student is to respond (option 5), whether to start with easy or difficult tasks (option 10), and whether to have students reply in complete sentences (option 24). But there are several others of the earlier options which should not be overlooked. One is whether to pre-teach the words that students use in making their suggestions (option 16): "(I think) you need a yellow rod," for example. Another is how to react to the students' errors of language (option 18).

Here are three such changes that you might make at step 3 of "Rod Technique 1":

3a. Students reply according to the form of your question – simply with the name of a color, or with some sentence frame provided by you: "You need a .... rod," "Put a .... rod," and so forth.
3b. Instead of letting students reply spontaneously, have them wait a few seconds until you give them the signal to respond (option 2b).
3c. Have students work in pairs (option 26b). Members of each pair consult each other but do not let them give their guesses until you call on them.

In preparing for the change from teacher to student initiative (option 8), have students do free recall (option 25b) of what you have used in turns 1 and 3, and write the results on the board so that students can draw from them (option 17a) in asking their questions.

Exercise 8.6

Rod Technique 2: "Robin Hood's Barn"

Goals: Linguistic: expanding students' ability to understand and then to use complex language about simple things. Functional: identification or specification.

Technique:
1. Build a configuration of two to five or more rods on the table. The configuration may represent something (building, car, person, etc.) or it may not, and it may be of any size and complexity.
2. Say something about one of the rods.
3. Students identify which of the rods you were talking about.

1. For which of options 1–30 (see list in the appendix) are the alternatives specified in "Rod Technique 2"?
2. For which options are additional alternatives available?

COMMENTS

By now the options should be pretty familiar to you. Here are a few possibilities that you may already have thought of: In step 1 of "Rod Technique 2," the configuration may be built either by you or by a student (option 8). It may be a simple and stable configuration or a precarious one, in which you add a new rod before moving to the next student. This is a form of dramatization (option 12b) which has frequently worked quite well for me. As you go on, you may move generally from right to left, top to bottom, and so on, or you may skip around (option 6). The change from one alternative of this option to another is something that students notice and respond to.

What is said may be very straightforward: "The blue rod." In general, however, it should be indirect (hence the name "Robin Hood's Barn"):
"the one at the end of the blue rod"
"the one underneath the dark green rod"
"the color of the sky"
"the one in the middle"
"the color of Jim's shirt"
"the one pointing toward the door"
"longer than the one with the color of grass"
"the color of the field on which the stars appear in the flag of the United States"
This is of course our familiar option 9 (hiding words) in full bloom.

There are many other options for which more than one alternative makes sense in this technique, but they need not be described here.

Among them are options 2–6, 10, 13, and 14 (see appendix). If you choose 8b (student initiative) combined with 25b (free recall), you can switch between the alternatives of 24 (linguistic form of replies), and you will almost certainly need to choose something from option 18 (responding to errors of language).

If you begin by doing the speaking yourself, you will take advantage of the fact that students can understand much more than they can produce. If you then move on to let students do the talking, you will take advantage of another fact – that people can take what they have just heard and build it into their own repertoire.

This activity lends itself to another option which is available with many of the activities that were described in Chapters 2–7:

OPTION 31: WHETHER THE PACE OF THE ACTIVITY SHOULD BE RELAXED OR HARD-DRIVING

a. Aim for relaxed smoothness. Advantage: This is less tiring on everyone, and less intimidating to those who lack confidence.
b. Aim for a rapid, almost staccato rhythm. You may even want to count the number of correct responses that the class can produce in a one- or two-minute period of time and write the number on the board so that the class can try to better its own record. Advantages: (i) A little of this can be invigorating, and if it goes smoothly it can produce a pleasant kind of exhilarated concentration. (ii) It provides a simple shared goal which can become the occasion for developing team spirit. (This alternative was considered the ideal for drilling and dialog practice in much of the teaching that was done by the Audiolingual Method, more for the sheer number of responses than for any psychological effect on the students.)

Exercise 8.7

Rod Technique 3: "The Little Green Rod"

Goals: Linguistic: encouraging production by students on the basis of full nonverbal imagery, with gentle transition to correct language. Functional: verification.

Technique: This is a technique that I have written about elsewhere. I repeat it here because it is a maximally simple prototype of one important way of helping students to form full and vivid nonverbal images, and because it shows that rods can produce nonverbal imagery far beyond their lengths, colors, and relative positions.
1. Place one of the 3-cm green rods on the empty tabletop in front of a student.

2. In a quiet, reassuring tone of voice, say something like this: "I'd like you to look for a minute at this rod and visualize it as some kind of building – any kind of building. Then tell me about the building. I'll check and see if I'm getting the same picture that you have."
3. Whatever the student says, repeat the same *idea* (not the same *words*) in correct language. Make it clear that you are doing so in order to ask the student to verify the accuracy of your perception. From time to time, break in with a summary of what you have understood so far. After a minute or two, thank the student and give a final summary of what the student has described, again asking for verification.
4. The language that has been generated in steps 1–3 is now available for use in any of a number of ways: for writing on the board, for question-and-answer practice, for tape recording, for distribution in written form, and for many others.

1. Which alternatives does "Rod Technique 3" use from options 1–31 (see list in appendix)?
2. Which aspects of this technique are conducive to the formation of nonverbal images?

COMMENTS

Any reader working alone can easily generate a series of answers to question 1, and so this question does not require specific comment here. I think there is still considerable value in putting oneself through the discipline of answering it, though, and particularly in comparing one's answers with those of other teachers.

Although this technique uses the rods that are often associated with the Silent Way, it actually developed out of some of my exposure to Counseling-Learning. Time and again, it seems to have produced non-verbal images which are unusually full and vivid not only to the student who generated them, but also to his or her classmates. Here are some of my guesses about why it is so effective:
- The size, the proportions, and especially the color of this particular rod are all nonthreatening.
- The calm and reassuring voice of the teacher also works to lower inhibitions and anxiety.
- The visual simplicity of the rod on the empty tabletop makes concentration easy.
- The quiet, noncorrecting style of the teacher's response confirms the imagery that has been reported so far and makes it available as a basis for further visualization.
- Placing the student in the role of authority with regard to the facts gives the student confidence.

- The fact that the teacher is repeating the content in correct language prevents the anxiety that students are just being exposed to one another's imperfect language.

Pictures

Pictures, like rods, are nonverbal materials that can be useful in teaching verbal skills. Unlike rods they have been around for many generations, and there are numerous sets of them on the market. A book that is concerned with imagery needs to deal with pictures, but not because pictures are direct and dependable sources of visual images. Quite the opposite, in fact. Pictures are frequently deceptive with regard to the images that students derive from them, for two reasons. On the one hand, different people pick up different visual items from the same objective external stimulus. This is true even within a culture, and it is even more true when students and teacher bring with them different culturally determined perceptions and expectations. On the other hand, we must not forget to take into account the many nonvisual items of purpose, emotion, social relationship, and so on which any reasonably complex and interesting picture triggers. In everyday language we sometimes call a drawing or photograph an *image*, but I prefer to reserve that term for whatever is formed in the head of each student as a result of exposure to such a stimulus.

The materials that we will look at in this chapter are *Double Action Picture Cards*, designed by Jane Yedlin and drawn by Penny Carter (Addison-Wesley, 1981). I selected this set of pictures for three reasons. First of all, I have had numerous happy experiences with them in my own classes. Second, they are graphically simple black-and-white drawings. Finally, the "double-action" feature compounds the imagery-generating potential of the individual cards. Figure 8.1 contains one pair of pictures from the set.

Exercise 8.8

1. How would you use the first card from Lesson 3 (see Figure 8.1) with a class of people many of whom were almost but not quite absolute beginners in English?
2. What alternatives did you find yourself using from options 1–31?
3. Compare your answers with those of others.

Figure 8.1. Pictures from pages 22 (*top*) and 32 (*bottom*), Lessons 3 and 4, in *Double Action Picture Cards*, designed by Jane Yedlin and drawn by Penny Carter. The pictures have been reduced in size for reproduction here. (Reproduced with permisson. © 1981 by Addison-Wesley.)

COMMENTS

Double Action Picture Cards were among the materials that I was using with two beginning classes when the idea for this book first began to take shape. Here is a handout that I prepared for a group of inexperienced volunteer teachers as I tried to show them ways of getting the most out of the pictures.

a. ⟨1⟩ Before passing out any printed materials, show the students the picture. ⟨2⟩ Give them a full 60 seconds to look at it, and ⟨3⟩ even to come up and inspect it at close quarters if they like.

b. ⟨4⟩ Take a piece of chalk in your hand and go to the board. ⟨5⟩ Look inquiringly at the students, gesturing at the picture and at the empty board. ⟨6⟩ The students will begin to say things in Spanish or in English or both.

c. When you hear something in English, whether correct or not, ⟨7⟩ repeat it in an interested tone of voice and, if it is not too long, ⟨8⟩ write it on the board. (If you don't hear enough English, and if you understand something that someone has said in Spanish, ⟨9⟩ give the equivalent in correct English ⟨10⟩ in a tone of voice that is asking for confirmation that what you have said is indeed what the person meant.)

d. ⟨11⟩ Have one student come to the board at a time. ⟨12⟩ You read words off the board, and ⟨13⟩ the student points to them. In order to avoid a lot of shuffling back and forth, ⟨14⟩ have each student do this with five to ten words before being replaced by another student.

e. ⟨15⟩ Read words or phrases from the board and ⟨16⟩ have the class repeat in unison.

f. ⟨17⟩ Have one student at a time choose a word or phrase from the board and ⟨18⟩ say it aloud. ⟨19⟩ You repeat it correctly, but without giving any indication of whether the student's pronunciation was right. ⟨20⟩ Then the student repeats after you, making any corrections that he or she can. ⟨21⟩ You again give no indication of the quality of the student's pronunciation.

g. ⟨22⟩ You choose words or phrases from the board, and ⟨23⟩ let individuals repeat them after you. ⟨24⟩ Correct any errors, and give the individual one or two more chances if necessary.

Exercise 8.9

1. On the basis of what you have read in the earlier parts of this book, try to anticipate my comments on the numbered points in *a–g* in the previous exercise.
2. Compare your predictions with those of other members of your group.

COMMENTS

The numbers in ⟨ ⟩ were added during the writing of this chapter. They were not present or even thought of when the series was first used for teacher training.

Not all of the first 31 options are represented in this series of techniques: There is nothing to write or not to write in the students' books (option 1), no choice of linguistic registers (option 7), and no fixed sample of language which students are or are not to reproduce exactly (option 22).

A few alternatives apply throughout the series: the general approach is to move from simpler to more demanding tasks for the students (option 10a), students are at all times interacting with the teacher rather than with one another (option 19b), and they do not correct one another's work (option 26a). The whole series is an example of generating and briefly using material which is not in the book (option 21b). It is based on what students see in the picture rather than on what they are told to see, and so illustrates option 23b.

A few options are open throughout the series, and teachers should consider using one alternative after the other from the same option: whether to have students reply immediately or pause before replying (option 2); whether to call on students in fixed or in random order (option 4); how to designate which student is to respond (option 5); whether to move straight down the list that has accumulated on the board or to skip around (option 6); whether to put the words into short phrases when pronouncing them (option 9); whether to speak slowly or normally or indistinctly (option 14); and whether to have students reply in complete sentences (option 24). As I've already said, the value of using more than one alternative from the same option is that students respond to the change as a recognition that they have done one thing right and are ready for something new, and as a sign that the teacher is actively and imaginatively involved in what they are doing. If you choose to ask the students to reply in sentences, then you may or may not want to pre-teach the sentence frames that they will need for this purpose (option 16).

This series of techniques takes account of the fact that nonverbal images do not flow automatically from optical exposure to a picture ⟨1⟩, and that the formation of images requires time ⟨2⟩ and is helped by personal involvement ⟨3⟩. The picking up of the chalk ⟨4⟩ is a signal for the transition from nonverbal to verbal focus. The giving of this signal ⟨5⟩ is a function that is handled nonverbally (option 30b) so as to avoid disturbing students' concentration on the material that is being studied. The students use their existing resources ⟨17⟩ (option 15c) in order to exercise initiative (option 8b). The tones of voice suggested for ⟨7⟩ and ⟨10⟩ take the exchange out of the routine interaction between demanding teacher and compliant student, and so constitute a small but genuine example of option 12b. The use of writing ⟨8⟩ helps to stabilize the verbal imagery and to confirm or correct what students had gotten through their ears.

Many of the other options in the series as originally written are obvious and need not be listed here. It may be worth mentioning, however, that having the students come to the board and point to what the teacher says ⟨11–14⟩ is a means of overcoming one of the dangers in the use of option 8b in ⟨6⟩: Without these steps, student A may not be entirely sure of just what the word that student B contributed refers to.

Exercise 8.10

1. On the basis of your own judgment, which of the numbered points in the comments on exercise 8.8 would you like to omit or modify? It will probably be worthwhile to make written notes for your answer to this question before you:
2. Compare your ideas with those of others.

Exercise 8.11

1. Try writing a sequence like those in exercises 4.9 and 4.13 which embodies more than one alternative from each of several options.
2. Compare your results with those of others in your group.
3. What seemed to be the criteria for judging one combination of alternatives more suitable or more credible than another combination?

COMMENTS

In the last analysis, if in a particular class on a particular day a change from one alternative to another produces a small brightening of the eyes, and a sense that things are moving along nicely, then that change may be counted as suitable. If another combination, or the same combination in another class or in the same class on a different day, fails to produce those effects, than it must be judged unsuitable for that class under those circumstances. What has so often surprised me is to see how small a change can be and still work in this way.

Exercise 8.12

1. Look at the second picture in Figure 8.1. In each pair of *Double Action Pictures* there is one character who appears in both. There is also some kind of problem, conflict, or clear emotion. Who is the

recurring character in this pair? How would you describe the affective content?

2. What are the implications of these features of *Double Action Pictures*?

COMMENTS

Linguistically, the contrast between the two pictures provides meaningful support for all kinds of drills which involve pairs of clauses or short sentences: "The store is neat, but Stan's apartment is messy," "There's a window in Stan's apartment, but there isn't any window in the show-room," and so forth. Some of these pairs can illustrate the shortened patterns that we use when one element or another appears in both: "The store is neat, but Stan's apartment isn't," or "Stan was wearing a tie at work, but he isn't wearing *one* now."

The conflicts between the young couple who can't agree what to buy with their limited resources, and between Stan's desire to go out with his friend and his need to get his apartment under control, are ones with which many students will be able to identify. On a slightly deeper level, these pictures recognize the existence of painful discrepancies between public appearances and behind-the-scenes problems, and open the way for reference to such problems in the students' (and teacher's!) own lives.

These same pictures lend themselves to illustration of yet another option:

OPTION 32: WHETHER THE LESSON SHOULD STRIVE FOR SOMATIC EFFECTS

a. Try for somatic effects. The advantages are (i) that if you succeed, your material will be a lot easier for your students to recall, and (ii) that it's fun.

b. Don't try for somatic effects. The advantage here is that you avoid the risks of trying for them: (i) They take a certain amount of planning and effort. (ii) If they are not well-executed and mutually harmonious, they can be distracting.

The phrase *somatic effects* is admittedly obscure. It does *not* refer to having students carry out actions with their bodies – the kind of thing that Asher's Total Physical Response has exploited so well and so fully. That is also an option, and a very important one. What I mean by somatic effect, however, is illustrated by the graphic style of *Double Action Pictures*, which I find clear, vigorous, but also a bit crude. It looks as though the artist had used a great deal of physical energy in making the drawings, and relatively little thought. This is not a style with which I was initially as comfortable as I am with the more polished drawings that are found in most language textbooks. I quickly found out, though, that both my students and most of the other volunteer teachers responded with enthusiasm to the same features that had made me just a bit uneasy.

Somatic effects may be prompted by the drawings that we do for our classes, and by the style of handwriting that we use on the board. Some of the most exciting, however, are prompted by the language itself, in the use of rhyme and rhythm.

Exercise 8.13

1. Try your hand at making up simple rhythmic material, with or without rhyme, for presentation of sentences about one of the pictures in Figure 8.1.
2. Do the same for manipulative drills that are based on the contents of one or both of the pictures.

COMMENTS

Rhythm in this sense is much more specific and much more sharply focused than the more general *rhythm of class activity* that we talked about in exercise 3.6.

I once wrote jingles to go with several of the *Double Action Pictures*. Here are three of the four that went with this pair:

Stan:	*Carl or Ann:*
A TV?	
	Yes!
A blender?	
	No!
A toaster?	
	Maybe, but I don't think so!

Stan:	*Carl or Ann:*
Do you want to buy a fan?	
	I will next summer if I can!
Or a washer and a dryer?	
	No, the price has gotten higher!
Or a new refrigerator?	
	Not now. Maybe later!
Or a stove? How about it?	
	Maybe so, but I doubt it.
This mixer is on sale today!	
	No, I don't want it anyway!

156

Ben:	Stan:
Hey, Stan! Hey, Stan! Let's go have some fun!	Ben, can't you see I've got things to get done?
Hey, Stan! Hey, Stan! Let's go to the game!	Not now, Ben. Thanks just the same!
Hey, Stan! Hey, Stan! This is not like you!	I told you, Ben, I've got work to do!
Hey, Stan! Hey, Stan! It's getting late!	Ben, my mom is coming here at eight!

In writing this series of jingles I tried to restrict myself not only to very common words, but also to very common sentences – ones that in a city of 100,000 are probably used several times a day in exactly the form in which they appear in the jingles. My assumption was that memory for such sentences would be supported in three ways: by the verbal context, by the pictorial context, and by the physical patterns of rhyme and rhythm. I also found that my students seemed to enjoy the change of pace.

A drama technique

Alan Maley and Alan Duff's *Drama Techniques in Language Learning* (1982) is a full and ingenious exploration of what in this book we have been calling imagery. It is not a textbook for students, but a resource book for teachers. In this chapter we will look at only one of the hundreds of ideas that it contains.

Recognizing that the title of their book may be misleading, the authors are quick to point out that *drama* does not mean putting on plays before a passive audience or preparing for some great final performance. The activities they describe are dramatic in the sense that students use their own personalities in creating material and that what is done "draws on the unpredictable power generated when one person is brought together with others" for some purpose or combination of purposes (p. 6). The authors reject the common assumption that linguistic forms (words and grammatical patterns) must be created before the meanings (the non-verbal imagery) which they are to help to convey (p. 8). They believe that nonverbal images should often take shape before or through the words, and that "this other world does not need to be conjured up with

157

expensive equipment; all that is needed is a roomful of human beings"
(p. 15).

The technique that we will examine is called "Hotel Receptionist."
Here is an abridged version of the authors' description of it:

This activity includes two roles: a performer, played by one person, and a
receptionist, played by everyone else at once. The people who are the receptionists sit in a large horseshoe pattern, which represents the reception desk
of a hotel. The performer is to come to the desk and communicate some kind
of request. The gimmick is that the performer has lost his or her voice, and
so must use nonverbal means. [Presumably the performer is also for some
reason unable to write!]

At the start of one round of this activity, the performer receives a slip of
paper containing one or two sentences which state some request that a hotel
guest might need to make: "I want to book a long-distance call to Venice at
6 a.m. on Sunday. My room number is 101," or the like. The performer
looks at the request, memorizes it, and then moves to the open end of the
horseshoe. He or she continues miming until the receptionists have gotten the
exact wording of the request. Then another round starts, with another student in the performer role.

Exercise 8.14

Comment on this activity from the point of view of the generating of
verbal and nonverbal imagery, and then compare your observations with
those of others in your group.

COMMENTS

The task of the receptionist is made easier by the fact that the students
know what the setting and the roles are supposed to be. Instead of having
to draw on their total stock of nonverbal imagery based on all of their
life experiences, they find that a certain subset of this imagery has been
"primed" for them. This increases the efficiency of the exercise, at the
same time making it more vivid.

This activity allows for the three conditions that we have said are
necessary for the activation of appropriate networks and the formation
of the corresponding images (see exercise 2.3). The fact that the receptionist cannot possibly succeed without activating images derived from
previous experiences in hotels is the "occasion." Interesting outcomes
are provided not only by the final solution to the puzzle but also by the
performer's responses to each question from the receptionist. The authors warn that this is an activity which should not be rushed. It therefore
goes on long enough to allow sufficient time, and to ensure that the set

of nonverbal images generated will be sufficiently large and cohesive (see exercise 3.5).

Exercise 8.15

The authors label the "Hotel Receptionist" technique as suitable for students from the elementary level upward. How could you modify it so as to raise or lower the level of language proficiency that it requires?

COMMENTS

The most obvious way to change the level of difficulty is to change the message. The teacher has control both of the nature of the request (the nonverbal imagery to be conveyed) and of its wording (the verbal imagery that must be created in the receptionist). The two are at least partially independent of each other: "I need a towel" is verbally less demanding than "May I have a towel, please?" although the message is the same, and the message "May I have an extra bath towel, please?" contains meanings that are just beyond "May I have a towel?"

There is, however, another concern which many teachers have expressed in relation to relatively free-form conversational activities such as are found in *Drama Techniques*. Does not this kind of thing lead to the happy fixation of language habits which are less than sufficiently correct for the students' future needs? Maley and Duff too feel this concern. They concede (p. 14) that much of the language that is produced in drama activities is uncontrolled by the teacher, but feel that what is needed is "a balance between fluency and accuracy" rather than a permanent and unrelieved concern for the latter. They agree that "correct structures do need to be taught," but ask, "can they not be taught *meaningfully* from the very start?" (p. 9).

The authors themselves suggest that some of the linguistic material that is sure to be needed may be pre-taught (cf. option 16):

it's my turn...
what did he say?
wouldn't it be better if... ?
we didn't understand why...
[etc.]

These are examples of what in exercise 2.6 we called *flags*.

Further control of the language that students hear can be arranged by assuming that the performer does not understand the language of the receptionist without the aid of an interpreter, who is played by the teacher. The queries and guesses of the receptionist are repeated by the interpreter, thus both slowing the action down for the benefit of the weaker students and also providing a nonjudgmental confirmation or correction of whatever the students have said (option 18d, f). This is certainly a time for the teacher to enter fully into his or her role (option 12b) and perhaps even to make a few factual errors in translation (option 13b).

Exercise 8.16

Even with a single class at a given level of proficiency, the exploitation of options is still of potential value, just as it was with the other materials that we have looked at.

1. For which of options 1–32 are the alternatives pretty well fixed in "Hotel Receptionist"?
2. From which options would it be possible to select more than one alternative in this activity?

COMMENTS

According to the authors' directions, a round is not over until the receptionists have arrived at the exact wording on the slip of paper that was given to the performer (option 22a). It would be possible to conduct the first round or two according to option 22b, accepting solutions which include all of the facts but are worded a bit differently. Students in the receptionist role may be allowed to come out with their questions and guesses as they think of them (option 4b), or they may take turns (option 4a) so as to be sure that the action is not monopolized by those who are most loquacious and confident. As suggested in connection with exercise 8.12, even the most advanced classes may profit from occasionally using the teacher as interpreter, and when they do so, the teacher may make errors of fact.

Exercise 8.17

Maley and Duff called for a balance between accuracy and fluency, and we have noted the need for focus on verbal as well as on nonverbal imagery. How can an activity like "Hotel Receptionist" contribute toward the formation of accurate and reliable logogens?

COMMENTS

Aside from the use of the teacher as interpreter, students can profit from talking *about* an activity after they have finished participating *in* it. This is part of what Counseling-Learning calls the "reflection" phase (Curran

1976). If words and sentences are cited at this time, and relationships are described and illustrated, it is not empty verbal tokens that are being shuffled around. The linguistic forms still have attached to them the broad and rich emotional, purposive, and other items that were present during the enactment. The teacher may accept responsibility for providing appropriate citations from what has happened, but it may be better to have the students provide the citations through free recall (option 25). Material which is formally organized in this way but which still has fresh meanings attached to it should be ideal for many kinds of manipulative drill, which would be both dead and deadly if it were based on situations that existed only in the minds of the textbook writer and the teacher.

The value to be derived from exploring language structure through examination of recent and imaginally rich examples gives special importance to yet another option:

OPTION 33: WHETHER TO MAKE A TAPE RECORDING OF ACTIVITIES THAT CONTAIN SPONTANEOUS LANGUAGE

a. Don't make a tape recording. Advantages: (i) The recording may be acoustically indistinct. (ii) The mechanics of making the recording distract attention from what is going on during the activity. (iii) Playing the recording back takes as much time as the original activity.
b. Make a tape recording. Advantages: (i) Even though the recording may be indistinct, it still has an immediacy that can stimulate fuller recall of what was said. (ii) It is possible that many students absorb more from what they hear in their own voices than from what the teacher says.

COMMENTS

Acoustic quality can be improved by passing the microphone from person to person, as in the best-known technique of Community Language Learning (Curran 1972, 1976). If each person turns the machine on just before speaking and off immediately afterward, the resulting tape can be short and clear. Doing this takes some getting used to, but once students have gotten the hang of it, it moves pretty well. If the teacher is serving as interpreter, such a tape can be made rather easily.

Summary

The eight sets of materials at which we have looked in chapters 4–8 are only a small sample of the great variety of resources that are available to language teachers today. I hope that at least some of the specific suggestions I have given for using them will be of direct use to each reader, but my principal purpose in discussing them has been to develop and illustrate a set of principles – principles which in the long run will be of more value than any set of specific recommendations could ever be.

In conclusion, here is a set of comparisons that may help to clarify the message of this book:

IMAGERY

Items are more basic than the images which arise from them. An image is a one-time product of interaction between a set of stored networks of items and a set of stimuli derived from somewhere else.

OPTIONS

Options are more basic than the techniques or procedures to which they apply. A procedure is in fact a one-time product of the interaction between a teacher's internal stock of options and a set of external stimuli derived from the teacher's perception of the class.

(Compare the more usual assumption that *techniques* are the smallest exemplifications of *approach* and *methods*, in the terminology of Anthony 1963, or that *procedures* are the smallest exemplifications of *approach* and *design*, in the terminology of Richards and Rodgers 1986.)

The *spectrum of nonverbal memory items* that are relevant to language teaching is very broad, including particularly items of purpose and emotion.

The *range of choices* that faces us at any moment is also quite broad. The list of 33 given in this book is only partial.

(Although recent emphasis on communicative and functional teaching has drawn increased attention to the purposive and emotional dimensions, language teachers over the years have tended to think of meanings in terms of the five senses plus a few rudimentary distinctions of time and social status and the like.)

The teacher consciously works with the verbal and nonverbal *images* in the minds of students.

In order to work with the students' images, the teacher is constantly using and modifying his or her own images of what those images in the minds of the students are.

(This is not the same as simply following a technique, presenting material, and reacting to students' responses.)

| Students need to have a rich network of *parallel paths* between verbal and corresponding nonverbal items, whether those items are lexical or structural. | Teachers use a large number of *combinations of alternatives from a few options* in any one activity. |

(It is more usual to be satisfied with developing one quick and simple bond between a word and its meaning, or to have one or more basic techniques for conducting each type of activity.)

In the writing projects in which I have participated in the last three years, I have found these developing concepts of imagery to be increasingly useful. Similarly, observing myself with a beginning-level tutee in English during the last six weeks of the preparation of this manuscript, I have seen that I do in fact make spontaneous use of options pretty much as described here. So I am sure that this book is at least a fair description of what I do. I hope that individual readers have found that it fits with their own practice and perhaps expands it a bit. More important, I hope that it has stimulated mutually helpful comparisons of experiences and exchanges of thinking *among* readers. That is where the craft of teaching is learned best!

In the literature

Larsen-Freeman (1986) contains classroom episodes that illustrate a number of methods. I have seen the chapters on Grammar-Translation and Audiolingualism. The episodes are clear enough so that it would be an interesting exercise to try interpreting each of these methods in terms of imagery.

Raimes (1983) devotes a whole chapter to the use of pictures with special reference to the teaching of writing.

Among Caleb Gattegno's books, the ones known best to language teachers are *Teaching Foreign Languages in Schools* (1972) and *The Common Sense of Teaching Foreign Languages* (1976). He has more recently published *The Teaching and Learning of Foreign Languages* (1985). None of these contains as many techniques for using rods as teachers are likely to hope for, but the author feels (as I understand him) that it is better for people to work things out for themselves. He's probably right there, too! A few rod techniques are described in Chapters 5, 6, and 11 of Stevick (1980).

Two good books on the fundamentals of using pictures are Wright (1976) and McAlpin (1980). There are many treatments of communicative activities these days, among them Stanislawczyk and Yavener (1976), Moskowitz (1978), and Littlewood (1981).

The use of drama in a more usual sense of that word is treated in Via (1976).

The aggressive use of rhythm in language classes was pioneered by Graham (1978). Gabriel (1983) also makes ingenious use of somatic effects. In that connection, I can't resist including a quotation from Arthur Koestler's *The Act of Creation*, found on page 3 of Maley and Duff (1982):

Rhythm and rhyme, assonance and pun are not artificial creations, but vestigial echoes of primitive phases in the development of language, and of the even more primitive pulsations of living matter; hence our particular receptiveness for messages which arrive in a rhythmic pattern.

Appendix: Summary of the options

[Page numbers refer to the first occurrence of the option.]

Option 1: *Should students write in their books?*
a = yes; b = no   (p. 58)

Option 2: *How quickly should students respond to a cue from the teacher?*
a = immediately; b = after a short pause   (p. 59)

Option 3: *Should students respond in chorus or individually?*
a = chorally; b = individually   (p. 60)

Option 4: *In what order should the students respond?*
a = in a predictable order; b = in an unpredictable order   (p. 60)

Option 5: *How should the teacher designate the student who is to respond?*
a = by name; b = by gesture; c = designate before task; d = designate after task   (p. 61)

Option 6: *How should the teacher move through the materials?*
a = in a predictable way, thoroughly; b = in a predictable order, but not using all items every time; c = at random   (p. 62)

Option 7: *What register of language should the teacher use?*
a = maximally clear; b = natural but careful; c = natural and relaxed (p. 64)

Option 8: *Who should take the initiative?*
a = teacher; b = students   (p. 65)

Option 9: *Should the teacher hide (embed) the words that the activity is about?*
a = no; b = hide in short expressions; c = hide in longer expressions   (p. 66)

Option 10: *Should the teacher move generally from harder to easier or from easier to harder combinations of alternatives?*
a = from easier to harder; b = from harder to easier   (p. 66)

Option 11: *Should the teacher personalize the sentences or words that are being learned?*
a = use the material without attaching it to individual students; b = attach various parts of the material to different students   (p. 71)

Option 12: *Should the teacher dramatize the activity?*
a = "play it straight"; b = put the material into a brief role play   (p. 71)

Option 13: *Should the teacher make errors of fact?*
a = avoid making errors of fact; b = make occasional errors of fact   (p. 72)

Option 14: *How should the teacher use his or her voice?*
a = speak slowly and firmly; b = speak normally; c = speak rapidly and indistinctly   (p. 72)

Option 15: *What should the teacher assume about the students' ability?*

a = assume no ability either to produce or to comprehend; b = assume some ability to comprehend; c = assume comprehension and some production ability   (p. 73)

Option 16: *Should the teacher pre-teach certain words and phrases?*
a = yes; b = no   (p. 79)

Option 17: *Should students hear the material before they see it in printed form?*
a = no; b = yes   (p. 81)

Option 18: *How should the teacher respond to the correctness or incorrectness of students' language?*
a = ignore errors; b = correct errors directly; c = pretend not to understand an incorrect form; d = work the correct form into whatever you say next; e = give a verbal reward for correct answers; f = comment only when student makes a mistake   (p. 85)

Option 19: *With whom should the students talk?*
a = with one another; b = with the teacher   (p. 86)

Option 20: *Should a given part of the material be used in only one way, or in more than one way?*
a = in one way; b = in multiple ways   (p. 88)

Option 21: *Should the published materials be supplemented?*
a = no; b = yes   (p. 89)

Option 22: *Should students be expected to reproduce exactly the language in a given list or sample?*
a = yes; b = no   (p. 99)

Option 23: *Should questions ask for answers that are to be found in the sample text or for students' inferences and interpretations?*
a = answers come from text; b = questions ask for inferences and interpretations   (p. 101)

Option 24: *Should replies be in complete sentences or in sentence fragments?*
a = in complete sentences; b = in fragments   (p. 101)

Option 25: *Should the students be asked to do free recall?*
a = no; b = yes   (p. 104)

Option 26: *Should students attempt to correct or improve one another's work?*
a = no; b = yes   (p. 110)

Option 27: *Should enactments take place in front of the whole class or should each group perform for another group?*
a = in front of the whole class; b = for another group   (p. 111)

Option 28: *Should students memorize dialogs or other material?*
a = yes; b = no   (p. 130)

Option 29: *Should teacher and students use translation as a means of ensuring understanding?*
a = no; b = yes   (p. 142)

Option 30: *Should communicative functions be carried out through words or through actions only?*
a = through words; b = without words   (p. 145)

Option 31: *Should the pace of an activity be relaxed or hard-driving?*
a = relaxed and smooth; b = rapid, staccato   (p. 148)

Option 32: *Should the lesson strive for somatic effects?*
a = yes; b = no (p. 155)
Option 33: *Should activities that involve spontaneous language be tape-recorded?*
a = no; b = yes (p. 161)

References

Ahsen, Akhter. 1981. Imagery approach in the treatment of learning disability. *Journal of Mental Imagery* 5(2): 157–96.

1984. ISM: The triple code model for imagery and psychophysiology. *Journal of Mental Imagery* 8(4): 15–42.

Anderson, John R. 1984. Spreading activation. In Anderson and Kosslyn (eds.), 1984, pp. 61–90.

Anderson, John R., and Stephen M. Kosslyn (eds.). 1984. *Tutorials in Learning and Memory*. San Francisco: W. H. Freeman.

Anthony, E. A. 1963. Approach, method, and technique. *English Language Teaching* 17: 63–67.

Asher, J. J. 1982. *Learning Another Language Through Actions*. Los Gatos, Cal.: Sky Oaks Productions.

Berns, M. S. 1984. Functional approaches to language and language teaching: another look. In S. J. Savignon and M. S. Berns (eds.), *Initiatives in Communicative Language Teaching*, pp. 3–22. Reading, Mass.: Addison-Wesley.

Boyd, John, and Mary Ann Boyd. 1983. *Before Book One*. New York: Regents.

Bracken, B. A. 1981. Relative meaning-evoking ability of personalized and non-personalized sentences. *Journal of Mental Imagery* 5: 121–4.

Bransford, J. D. 1979. *Human Cognition*. Belmont, Cal.: Wadsworth.

Brown, David. 1983. Conversational cloze tests and conversational ability. *English Language Teaching Journal* 37(2): 158–61.

Brumfit, Christopher. 1984. *Communicative Methodology in Language Teaching: The Roles of Fluency and Accuracy*. Cambridge: Cambridge University Press.

Bugelski, B. R. 1982. Learning and imagery. *Journal of Mental Imagery* 6(1): 1–92.

Buschke, H. 1974. Spontaneous remembering after recall failure. *Science* (3 May): 579–81.

Celce-Murcia, Marianne. 1985. Making informed decisions about the role of grammar in language teaching. *TESOL Newsletter* 19(1): 1–3.

Chaudron, Craig. 1983. Simplification of input: reinstatements and their effects on L2 learners' recognition and recall. *TESOL Quarterly* 17(3): 437–58.

Ciccone, D. S. 1973. Massed and distributed item repetition in item discrimination. *Journal of Experimental Psychology* 101: 396–7.

Cook, V. J. 1982. Structure drills and the language learner. *Canadian Modern Language Review* 38(2): 321–9.

Curran, Charles A. 1972. *Counseling-Learning: A Whole-Person Model for Education*. New York: Grune and Stratton.

References

1976. *Counseling-Learning in Second Languages*. Apple River, Ill.: Apple River Press.

Dickel, M. J., and S. Slak. 1983. Imaging vividness and memory for verbal material. *Journal of Mental Imagery* 7(1): 121–6.

Diller, Karl C. 1978. *The Language Teaching Controversy*. Rowley, Mass.: Newbury House.

Dirven, Rene, and J. Oakeshott-Taylor. 1985. Listening comprehension. A two-part "state-of-the-art-article." *Language Teaching* 17(4): 326–43 and 18(1): 2–20.

Ellis, Rod. 1982. Informal and formal approaches to communicative language teaching. *English Language Teaching Journal* 36(2): 73–81.

Ferreira, Linda. 1984. *Transitions*. Rowley, Mass.: Newbury House.

Finocchiaro, Mary, and C. Brumfit. 1983. *The Functional-Notional Approach: From Theory to Practice*. London: Oxford University Press.

Gabriel, Gary. 1983. *Rhyme and Reason*. New York: Regents.

Galyean, Beverley. 1977. A confluent design for language teaching. *TESOL Quarterly* 11: 142–56.

Gattegno, Caleb. 1972. *Teaching Foreign Languages in Schools: The Silent Way*. New York: Educational Solutions.

1976. *The Common Sense of Teaching Foreign Languages*. New York: Educational Solutions.

1985. *The Teaching and Learning of Foreign Languages*. Chapter 13 of *The Science of Education*. New York: Educational Solutions.

Gerngross, G., and H. Puchta. 1984. Beyond notions and functions: language teaching or the art of letting go. In S. J. Savignon and M. S. Berns (eds.), *Initiatives in Communicative Language Teaching*, pp. 89–108. Reading, Mass.: Addison-Wesley.

Graham, Carolyn. 1978. *Jazz Chants*. New York: Oxford University Press.

Greenwald, M. Jane. 1981. Developing and using cloze materials to teach reading. *Foreign Language Annals* 14(3): 185–8.

Grellet, Françoise. 1981. *Developing Reading Skills: A Practical Guide to Reading Comprehension Exercises*. Cambridge: Cambridge University Press.

Grossberg, Stephen. 1978. A theory of human memory. *Progress in Theoretical Biology* 5: 233–374.

Hamilton, Vernon. 1983. *The Cognitive Structures and Processes of Human Motivation and Personality*. Chichester: Wiley.

Harmer, Jeremy. 1982. What is communicative? *English Language Teaching Journal* 36(3): 164–8.

1983. *The Practice of English Language Teaching*. London: Longman.

Heilenman, L. K. 1983. The use of a cloze procedure in foreign language placement. *Modern Language Journal* 67(2): 121–6.

Jones, Leo, and C. von Baeyer. 1983. *Functions of American English: Communication Activities for the Classroom*. New York: Cambridge University Press.

Kimbrough, Victoria, Michael Palmer, and Donn Byrne. 1983. *Odyssey*. New York: Longman.

Krashen, S. D., and T. Terrell. 1983. *The Natural Approach: Language Acquisition in the Classroom*. London: Pergamon.

Lacasa, Judith, and Jaime Lacasa. 1983. Student-perceived communication needs: infrastructure of the functional/notional syllabus. *Foreign Language Annals* 16(3): 179–88.

Larsen-Freeman, Diane. 1986. *Techniques and Principles in Language Teaching.* New York: Oxford University Press.

Littlewood, William. 1981. *Communicative Language Teaching: An Introduction.* Cambridge: Cambridge University Press.

Lougheed, Lin. 1985. *Listening Between the Lines: A Cultural Approach.* Reading, Mass.: Addison-Wesley.

McAlpin, Janet. 1980. *The Magazine Picture Library.* London: Allen and Unwin.

McArthur, Tom. 1983. *A Foundation Course for Language Teachers.* Cambridge: Cambridge University Press.

Maley, Alan, and Alan Duff. 1982. *Drama Techniques in Language Learning,* new ed. Cambridge: Cambridge University Press.

Marks, D. F. 1984. The new structural approach to image formation, psychophysiology and psychopathology. *Journal of Mental Imagery* 8(4): 95–104.

Meredith, R. Alan. 1978. Improved oral test scores through delayed response. *Modern Language Journal* 62(7): 321–6.

Met, Myriam. 1984. Listening comprehension and the young second language learner. *Foreign Language Annals* 17(5): 519–23.

Morrison, D. M., and G. Low. 1983. Monitoring and the second language learner. In J. C. Richards and R. W. Schmidt (eds.), *Language and Communication*, pp. 228–50. New York: Longman.

Morton, J. 1969. Interaction of information in word recognition. *Psychological Review* 76: 165–78.

Morton, J., and K. Patterson. 1980. A new attempt at interpretation: or, an attempt at a new interpretation. In M. Coltheart, K. Patterson, and J. C. Marshall (eds.), *Deep Dyslexia*, pp. 91–100. London: Routledge and Kegan Paul.

Moskowitz, G. 1978. *Caring and Sharing in the Foreign Language Class.* Rowley, Mass.: Newbury House.

Norman, D. A. 1982. *Learning and Memory.* San Francisco: W. H. Freeman.

Oller, John. 1983. Story writing principles and ESL teaching. *TESOL Quarterly* 17(1): 39–54.

Oller, John, and Patricia Richard-Amato (eds.). 1983. *Methods That Work.* Rowley, Mass.: Newbury House.

Omaggio, Alice. 1982. The relationship between personalized classroom talk and teacher effectiveness ratings: some research results. *Foreign Language Annals* 14(4): 255–69.

Paivio, A., J. C. Yuille, and S. A. Madigan. 1968. Concreteness, imagery and meaningfulness values for 925 nouns. *Journal of Experimental Psychology Monograph* 76 (1, pt. 2): 1–25.

Paulston, C., and M. Bruder. 1975. *From Substitution to Substance: A Handbook of Structural Pattern Drills.* Rowley, Mass.: Newbury House.

Raimes, A. 1983. *Techniques in Teaching Writing.* New York: Oxford University Press.

Richards, Jack C. 1985. Listening comprehension: approach, design, and procedure. In Richards, *The Context of Language Teaching*, pp. 189–207.

References

New York: Cambridge University Press.

Richards, Jack C., and Theodore S. Rodgers. 1986. *Approaches and Methods in Language Teaching: A Description and Analysis.* New York: Cambridge University Press.

Rivers, Wilga. 1983. *Communicating Naturally in a Second Language.* New York: Cambridge University Press.

Rivers, Wilga, and Mary Temperley. 1978. *A Practical Guide to the Teaching of English as a Second or Foreign Language.* New York: Oxford University Press.

Schank, R. C. 1982. *Dynamic Memory: A Theory of Reminding and Learning in Computers and People.* Cambridge: Cambridge University Press.

Soudek, Lev, and Miluse Soudek. 1983. Cloze after 30 years: new uses in language teaching. *English Language Teaching Journal* 37(4): 335–40.

Stanislawczyk, Irene, and Symond Yavener. 1976. *Creativity in the Language Classroom.* Rowley, Mass.: Newbury House.

Stevick, E. W. 1980. *Teaching Languages: A Way and Ways.* Rowley, Mass.: Newbury House.

1982. *Teaching and Learning Languages.* Cambridge: Cambridge University Press.

Stevick, Paul R. 1923. *Success in Study for Freshmen.* Sioux City, Iowa: Morningside College.

Swan, Michael. 1985. A critical look at the Communicative Approach. *English Language Teaching Journal* 39(1): 2–12.

van Ek, J. A. 1977. *The Threshold Level for Modern Language Learning in Schools.* London: Longman.

van Parreren, C. F., and M. C. Schouten-van Parreren. 1981. Contextual guessing: a trainable reader strategy. *System* 9(3): 235–41.

Via, Richard. 1976. *English in Three Acts.* Honolulu: University Press of Hawaii.

Vigil, N. A., and John Oller. 1976. Rule fossilization: a tentative model. *Language Learning* 26(2): 281–96.

Warren, D. A. 1972. Stimulus encoding and memory. *Journal of Experimental Psychology* 94(1): 90–100.

1974. Association, directionality and stimulus encoding. *Journal of Experimental Psychology* 102(1): 151–8.

Whitaker, Sidney. 1983. Comprehension questions: about face! *English Language Teaching Journal* 37(4): 329–34.

Widdowson, Henry. 1983. *Learning Purpose and Language Use.* London: Oxford University Press.

Wilson, Virginia, and B. Wattenmaker. 1980a. *A Guidebook for Teaching ESL.* Boston: Allyn and Bacon.

1980b. *A Guidebook for Teaching Foreign Language: Spanish, French and German.* Boston: Allyn and Bacon.

Wright, Andrew. 1976. *Visual Materials for the Language Teacher.* London: Longman.

Wright, Andrew, D. Betteridge, and M. Buckby. 1984. *Games for Language Learning,* 2nd ed. Cambridge: Cambridge University Press.

Yedlin, Jane. 1981. *Double Action Picture Cards.* Reading Mass.: Addison-Wesley.

Index

Index

Index

van Ek, J. A., 35
van Parreren, C. F., 52
verbal items and imagery, 8, 15, 19,
    24, 41, 43, 44, 88, 101, 109,
    121, 131, 154, 158, 164
verbal vs. nonverbal, 8, 24, 131, 163
Via, Richard, 164
Vigil, N. A., 92
visualization, 3
voice of teacher, 35, 72, 85, 149,
    153
  see also option 14

Warren, D. A., 51
Wattenmaker, Beverly, 52
Widdowson, Henry, 19
Wilson, Virginia, 52
word list, English and Swahili (ex-
    ample), 6
Wright, Andrew, 77, 137, 164
writing in books, *see* option 1

Yavener, S., 165
Yedlin, J., 150
Yuille, J. C., 51